Study Guide for David _____

AMERICA:

The Politics of Diversity

Brian L. Fife
Indiana University-Purdue University
at Fort Wayne

West/Wadsworth
I⊕P® An International Thomson Publishing Company

Belmont, CA • Albany, NY • Boston • Cincinnati • Johannesburg • London • Madrid • Melbourne
Mexico City • New York • Pacific Grove, CA • Scottsdale, AZ • Singapore • Tokyo • Toronto

For more information, contact Wadsworth Publishing Company, 10 Davis Drive, Belmont, CA 94002, or electronically at http://www.wadsworth.com.

International Thomson Publishing Europe
Berkshire House
168-173 High Holborn
London, WC1V 7AA, United Kingdom

International Thomson Editores
Seneca, 53
Colonia Polanco
11560 México D.F. México

Nelson ITP, Australia
102 Dodds Street
South Melbourne
Victoria 3205 Australia

International Thomson Publishing Asia
60 Albert Street #15-01
Albert Complex
Singapore 189969

Nelson Canada
1120 Birchmount Road
Scarborough, Ontario
Canada M1K 5G4

International Thomson Publishing Southern Africa
Building 18, Constantia Square
138 Sixteenth Road, P.O. Box 2459
Halfway House, 1685 South Africa

International Thomson Publishing Japan
Hirakawa-cho Kyowa Building, 3F
2-2-1 Hirakawa-cho
Chiyoda-ku
Tokyo 102, Japan

ISBN 0-534-54865-2

CONTENTS

PREFACE

This study guide is designed to assist students in understanding the central themes and issues in *America: The Politics of Diversity*. In order to maximize comprehension of the text, all aspects of the study guide should be fully utilized by students. Each chapter includes the following sections:

Summary (a concise overview of the chapter);

Outline (this obviously reflects the major headings of each of the textbook chapters with corresponding page references);

Key Terms, Concepts, Events, and People (includes the glossary terms included in the text with the appropriate page references);

Practice Exam (this includes a multiple choice and essay section, and is designed to test students' level of understanding of the text);

Critical Thinking Exercises (this section is designed to challenge students by applying chapter concepts to contemporary issues and/or events); and

Answers (for both the multiple choice and essay exams–the essay responses are fairly brief, but should provide students with the overall basis of a concrete response).

Space is provided for student responses for the Key Terms, Concepts, Events, and People section. Depending on the students' handwriting style and the term itself, more or less space may actually be needed to respond fully. If used copiously by students, this study guide should prove to be an effective tool for understanding *America: The Politics of Diversity*.

Students should also be aware that Wadsworth has created many other student-oriented products to assist in understanding American government. These include a CD-ROM, InfoTrac (an on-line library with current articles available 24 hours a day), a reader, a critical thinking guide, a Handbook of Selected Legislation, a Handbook of Selected Court Cases, as well as a web site for the text). Students are urged to integrate all of these items into their educational experience.

Brian L. Fife
Indiana University-Purdue University at Fort Wayne

CHAPTER 1
EXPLAINING AMERICAN GOVERNMENT

I.   Summary

Since diversity is deeply embedded in American history, it is integrated throughout this introductory text in American Politics. This is why the author entitled the book *America: The Politics of Diversity*. Terms such as political power, government, political legitimacy, and political system are explained so that students will develop a better understanding of American history, a better grasp on contemporary politics, and more insight into future challenges. By many criteria (e.g., political culture, race, ethnicity, subnational economies, regionalism, and political ideology), the United States is a very diverse society. As such, political scientists have created many different theories to explain American politics. Among them are democratic theory, elite theory, pluralism, and hyperpluralism. While elements of each theory can be identified in American society, hyperpluralism is becoming increasingly evident. Along with diversity, hyperpluralism affects many aspects of American government including its structure, behavior, institutions, and public policies.

II.   Outline

III.   Key Terms, Concepts, Events, and People

Be able to identify and/or define each of the following and state its importance in a short paragraph.

Power (p.4)

Political power (p.4)

Government (p.4)

Public policy (p.4)

Political legitimacy (p.4)

Political system (p.5)

Political environment (p.5)

Linkage institutions (p.5)

Conversion process (p.5)

3

IV. Practice Exam

(Answers appear at the end of this chapter)

Multiple Choice

1. The study of politics is the study of
   A. politicians.
   B. power.
   C. abortion politics.
   D. social relationships.

2. For centuries, European monarchs claimed to have
   A. the divine right to rule.
   B. a popular mandate to govern.
   C. supernatural powers.
   D. the right to hire or fire the Pope.

3. In 1996, American voters
   A. elected a Democratic president.
   B. elected a Republican Congress.
   C. selected unified party government.
   D. Both a + b.

4. There are _____ different "governments" in the United States.
   A. 51
   B. 117
   C. more than 87,000
   D. more than 500,000

5. Currently, about _____ percent of the U.S. population is Hispanic.
   A. 4
   B. 8
   C. 10
   D. 25

6. Currently, about _____ percent of the U.S. population is African American.
   A. 4
   B. 12
   C. 21
   D. 30

7. Currently, about _____ percent of the U.S. population is Caucasian?
   A. 45
   B. 60
   C. 74
   D. 86

8. By 2010, which of the following states will NOT have a majority of minorities?
   A. California
   B. Texas
   C. Maine
   D. Hawaii

9. How would you describe the current economy in the United States?
   A. It is a manufacturing-based economy.
   B. It is a post-industrial economy.
   C. It is an economy where the "knowledge workers" receive low pay.
   D. It is an economy where the "bottom tier" receives high pay.

10. Which of the following is TRUE about contemporary liberals?
   A. They oppose government intervention across the board.
   B. They favor a governmental role in regulating business.
   C. They oppose government-imposed limits on personal liberty.
   D. Both b + c.

11. Which of the following is TRUE about contemporary conservatives?
    A. They oppose government intervention across the board.
    B. They consistently favor government regulation on behalf of the "common people."
    C. They favor less government in providing social services and protecting civil liberties.
    D. They oppose government regulation on social issues like abortion.

12. The Greek philosopher Aristotle
    A. believed that all citizens were equal.
    B. believed that slaves and women should be excluded from participating in politics.
    C. believed that all people should have the right to vote.
    D. believed that New England town meetings should be abolished.

13. When the Framers wrote the Declaration of Independence
    A. they believed that all citizens were equal.
    B. they believed that slavery should be abolished.
    C. they believed that the phrase "all men are created equal" meant white males with property.
    D. they believed that women should have the right to vote.

14. Local power structures include
    A. the media.
    B. interest group leaders.
    C. powerful individuals.
    D. All of the above.

15. _____ defined the term "faction" in *The Federalist*, No. 10.
    A. James Madison
    B. Alexis de Tocqueville
    C. Robert Dahl
    D. C. Wright Mills

16. In a hyperpluralistic system,
    A. political gridlock is the norm.
    B. power is thinly scattered.
    C. Both a + b.
    D. power is concentrated in the hands of a few.

17. Which of the following statements is TRUE about American society?
    A. Americans strongly support the the concept of individualism.
    B. Americans tend to put their community needs above their own.
    C. American individualism is accepted by both the ideological left and right.
    D. Both a + c.

18. Why are few public officials elected with a true majority?
    A. Multiple candidacies.
    B. Low voter turnout.
    C. Millions of Americans are not registered to vote.
    D. All of the above.

19. About 35 million Americans
    A. live at the local level.
    B. live under private governments such as homeowners associations.
    C. live in civil societies.
    D. live in a diverse country.

20. Who is famous for saying that "all politics is local?"
    A. George Washington
    B. Abraham Lincoln
    C. Tip O'Neill
    D. Ronald Reagan

21. Identify and detail all the steps of the public policy making process.
22. Explain why the United States is a multiracial and multiethnic society.
23. What is a political ideology? Identify and distinguish between and among the four predominant ideologies in the United States today.
24. What are the four main political theories used to explain American politics? Be sure to define each theory and provide a general critique of them as well.
25. What are the six conditions present in American politics that help to support the hyperpluralism theory? Detail each one.

V. Critical Thinking Exercises

1. By any comparative criteria, the United States is a diverse society. In your opinion, how does this enhance American society, and how does it challenge the system simultaneously?

2. One of the most important questions to ask when discussing political ideology is the following: what is the proper role of the federal government in society? Identify five critical issues (e.g., domestic economy, crime, health care, education, environment and so forth) in American society, and try to ascertain what role the federal government should play with regard to these issues. Upon doing so, try to assess your own political ideology. Would you label yourself a liberal, conservative, libertarian, populist or something else?

VI. Answers to the Practice Exam

1.	B	11.	C
2.	A	12.	B
3.	D	13.	C
4.	C	14.	D
5.	C	15.	A
6.	B	16.	C
7.	C	17.	D
8.	C	18.	D
9.	B	19.	B
10.	D	20.	C

21. There are four primary steps in the public policy making process. The first step is agenda setting. This occurs when many people debate a particular problem or concern. Policy makers, political actors, key individuals, interest groups, and the media all play a role in this initial stage. The second stage of the process is policy formation. This entails the creation of policy proposals to solve or address a problem or concern. Proposals come in many different forms (i.e., congressional bills, executive orders, judicial decisions, and agency rulings among others). In the third stage, policy adoption, specific proposals are selected or rejected by policy makers. Most people associate this stage when the president signs a bill, Congress passes a law, or the Supreme Court announces a decision, but policies are adopted in many other ways as well. Finally, an approved policy is carried out in the fourth stage, policy implementation and evaluation. After a policy is put into effect, it is subsequently evaluated which involves determining whether or not the policy is working. After evaluation, policies may be continued, changed, or abolished altogether.

22. A demographical examination of the United States demonstrates that it is a multiracial and multiethnic society. In a nation of approximately 270 million citizens, about 74 percent are white, 12 percent are

African American, 10 percent are Hispanic, 3 percent are Asian or Pacific Islander, and less than 1 percent are Native American. In the decades to come, the Caucasian majority will shrink in proportion due to its declining birth rates and the in-migration of nonwhites. By 2010, California, Texas, New York, Florida, New Mexico, and Hawaii are projected to have a majority of "minority" citizens. As minority populations grown, they will undoubtedly increase their political strength. This will likely result in more conflict between the white and nonwhite populations. Complicating matters even more is the intermarriage of diverse racial and ethnic groups. More and more families are becoming multiracial, which adds to the diversity present in the United States.

23.   A political ideology is a coherent view of what government should be doing and how it should be doing it. The four predominant ideologies in America today are liberalism, conservatism, libertarianism, and populism. Liberals favor a governmental role in regulating business, providing social services, and protecting civil liberties, especially for the disadvantaged in society. Conservatives typically advocate a minimal amount of governmental involvement in those areas. Yet liberals and conservatives alike contradict their own respective philosophies on social issues like abortion. Liberals oppose any governmental regulation on personal liberty issues while conservatives advocate governmental restrictions on the abortion procedure. Libertarians oppose government intervention across the board and populists favor government regulation on behalf of common citizens.

24.   The four main political theories used to explain American politics are democratic theory, elite theory, pluralist theory, and hyperpluralism. Each explores the following question: who governs and what difference does it make? According to traditional democratic theory, all of us govern in a sense. There are two different forms of democracy: participatory democracy and representative democracy. Participatory democracy envisions rule by the many. Representative democracy suggests rule by the few on behalf of the many. In a republic like the United States, policy makers may negotiate and compromise with each other, but they are held accountable by the people. Some scholars maintain that traditional democratic theory advances political ideals better than it describes political reality. They raise some very difficult questions for democratic theorists. Does a representative democracy assume greater citizen interest than is often the case? Do elected officials represent everyone or rather those who vote or those who can afford to lobby them? Democratic theory seemingly has a difficult time accounting for the relationship between government and wealth and the persistence of inequality in society. Elite theorists believe that all societies naturally divide into two classes: the few who rule and the many who do not. Elite power structures exist at all levels of government, and the wealthy and powerful dominate policy making. As compelling as this theory is to many people, it does not fully explain American politics. Many businesses of all sizes compete for power, so the elites do not have monolithic policy objectives. Because elites tend to focus largely on economic issues, they do not contribute to many other important policy debates in the United States. Pluralists contend that no single group dominates policy making all the time, and they believe in group politics. At all levels of government, pluralists believe that groups representing a multitude of interests attempt to influence public policy making, and the policies that are enacted tend to reflect the diversity present in society. Yet not all politics can be labeled "group" politics. Group competition cannot explain why certain individuals tend to wield a great deal of political influence. Also, the American political system itself tends to limit group power and success to some extent. Lastly, pluralism suggests an equilibrium exists among competing groups. If that were true, then millions would not be complaining about political gridlock. The newest approach to explaining American politics is hyperpluralism. Hyperpluralism is a term used to describe the American political system today, where the number of interest groups has increased dramatically over the last three decades. Those who believe in this theory suggest that the expansion of groups in society has resulted in increased political gridlock. The textbook author suggests that while hyperpluralism does not explain all American politics fully, it increasingly makes sense in understanding the political system in the United States.

25.   There are six conditions present in American politics that help to support the hyperpluralism theory.

These include the constancy of individualism, group particularity, cultural pluralism, fading majoritarianism, enduring localism, and jurisdictional fragmentation. Hyperpluralism could not be present without individualism. Americans have always stressed personal autonomy at the expense of commitment to a larger community. As groups have grown in number, they have become more particular. More and more interest groups are focused on single issue politics, which makes it difficult for policy makers to address their needs without incurring the wrath of other groups. In addition, the United States is becoming a more culturally diverse society, as the dominant Caucasian population is shrinking as a percentage of the whole. More evidence of hyperpluralism is the changing nature of majority rule, which is a major principle in American politics. The Framers of the Constitution believed that, in a representative democracy, elected officials would approximate the views of the majority. Yet as groups multiply in number, it becomes more difficult to assess the larger public interest. Fading majoritarianism is not simply limited to national politics. It is still at the local level where people live and work. The diversity present in the United States literally exists in the local communities. Lastly, the final evidence of hyperpluralism is jurisdictional fragmentation. In the U.S. Constitution, power is shared between and among the three branches of governments (legislative, executive, and judicial) and between the national and state governments. This insures constant struggles in the American political system and a good deal of political gridlock as well.

CHAPTER 2
AMERICAN CONSTITUTIONAL DEVELOPMENT

I. Summary

The Framers of the Constitution created a limited government where the ultimate sovereigns, the people, would elect representatives to serve on their behalf. They also stressed the values of individual liberty and equality. The Constitution can be viewed as a careful balance between the failure of the Articles of Confederation and a confederal form of government and the British model of government with a strong central government. The Framers perceived that a strong central government would result in tyranny and an infringement of individual liberties, and that a very weak central government resulted in economic chaos and unsavory rivalries between and among the states. As a result, the Framers created a federal system of government where power was shared between the national government and the states. Most of the political issues that are addressed in the Constitution (e.g., the structure of the legislative branch, representation in the U.S. House of Representatives, and presidential selection) fueled extensive political debates and resulted in compromise. Once the Framers drafted the Constitution, it had to be ratified by at least nine of the thirteen states. As a result, the proponents of the Constitution, the federalists, produced the Federalist Papers and ratification occurred. The core principles of the Constitution are popular sovereignty, rule of law, republicanism, federalism, separation of powers, checks and balances, and individual rights. The Constitution can be changed by a formal amendment, via judicial interpretation, and by cultural change and diversity.

II. Outline

The Constitution in Action: Bombs and Freedom (p.27)
The Journey Toward a Constitution (p.28)
       The Idea of Constitutionalism (p.28)
       Colonial Constitutionalism (p.29)
       Native American Influences (p.30)
       Lessons of Colonial America (p.31)
       Seeds of Revolution (p.32)
Crafting a Constitution (p.33)
       The Failure of Confederation (p.33)
       The Art of Compromise in Philadelphia (p.35)
       The Ratification Campaign (p.38)
Constitutional Basics (p.40)
       The Preamble (p.40)
       The Principles (p.40)
The Living Constitution (p.42)
Women's Rights and the Living Constitution (p.44)
Constitutionalism, Diversity, and Hyperpluralism (p.46)
Conclusion (p.47)

III. Key Terms, Concepts, Events, and People

Be able to identify and/or define each of the following and state its importance in a short paragraph.

Constitutionalism (p.28)

Classical liberalism (p.28)

Social contract (pp.28-29)

Declaration of Independence (p.29)

Magna Carta (p.29)

Mayflower Compact (p.29)

Iroquois League (p.31)

Federalism (p.31)

Federal system (p.31)

Unitary system (p.31)

Common law (p.32)

Mercantilism (p.32)

Second Continental Congress (p.33)

Articles of Confederation (p.33)

Shays' Rebellion (p.34)

Constitutional convention (p.34)

Virginia Plan (p.36)

New Jersey Plan (p.36)

Supremacy clause (p.37)

Great or Connecticut Compromise (p.37)

Three-Fifths Compromise (p.37)

Electoral College (p.38)

Federalists (p.38)

Anti-federalists (p.38)

Popular sovereignty (p.40)

Republic (p.40)

Republicanism (p.41)

Separation of powers (p.41)

Checks and balances (p.41)

Equal protection clause (p.42)

Incorporation doctrine (p.42)

Formal amendment process (p.43)

Judicial interpretation (p.43)

Marbury v. Madison (1803) (p.43)

Equal Rights Amendment (ERA) (p.45)

Judicial federalism (p.47)

IV.   Practice Exam

(Answers appear at the end of this chapter)

Multiple Choice

1. In writing the Declaration of Independence, Thomas Jefferson borrowed ideas from

   _____.
   - A.   Aristotle
   - B.   Plato
   - C.   John Locke
   - D.   Ralph Waldo Emerson

2. Members of the British nobility forced King John to sign the Magna Carta in _____.
   - A.   1215
   - B.   1557
   - C.   1607
   - D.   1712

3. _____ was a union of six Indian peoples.
   - A.   The Jamestown League
   - B.   The Iroquois League
   - C.   The Seminole League
   - D.   The Penabscot League

4. The Boston Tea Party occurred in _____.
   - A.   1763
   - B.   1773
   - C.   1783
   - D.   1793

5. _____ advocated independence from Great Britain in *Common Sense*.
   - A.   Thomas Jefferson
   - B.   Samuel Adams
   - C.   Ralph Waldo Emerson
   - D.   Thomas Paine

6. Which of the following is TRUE about the Articles of Confederation?
   - A.   The Articles created a national Congress with the power to coin money.
   - B.   The Articles created a weak president.
   - C.   The Articles created a strong federal judiciary.
   - D.   The Articles created an effective national government.

7. _____ directed the Annapolis Convention in 1786.
   - A.   George Washington
   - B.   James Madison
   - C.   Alexander Hamilton
   - D.   John Marshall

8. Which event demonstrated the ineffectiveness of the federal government during the Articles of Confederation?
   - A.   Whisky Rebellion
   - B.   Boston Tea Party
   - C.   Alien and Sedition Acts
   - D.   Shays' Rebellion

9. _____ delegates attended the Philadelphia Convention.
   - A.   26
   - B.   55
   - C.   280
   - D.   567

10. _____ argued that the Framers were an economic elite which wanted a strong government to promote commerce, private property, and economic stability.
   - A.   Charles Beard
   - B.   George Mason
   - C.   Patrick Henry
   - D.   Edmund Randolph

11. Under the Virginia Plan, which states would have monopolized the new Congress?
 A. Rhode Island, Massachusetts, and Connecticut.
 B. Massachusetts, Pennsylvania, and Virginia.
 C. New York, Virginia, and South Carolina.
 D. New Jersey, Maryland, and North Carolina.

12. The U.S. Constitution was written in _____.
 A. 1781
 B. 1787
 C. 1789
 D. 1791

13. What was the biggest objection to the U.S. Constitution after it was written?
 A. It created a president for life.
 B. It gave most of the political power to the U.S. Supreme Court.
 C. It lacked a list of individual rights and liberties.
 D. It did not abolish slavery.

14. Under the original Constitution, U.S. senators
 A. were elected by the people.
 B. were selected by state governors.
 C. were selected by members of the U.S. House of Representatives.
 D. were selected by state legislatures.

15. Article I of the U.S. Constitution created
 A. the legislative branch.
 B. the executive branch.
 C. the judicial branch.
 D. political parties and interest groups.

16. The Bill of Rights was added to the U.S. Constitution in _____.
 A. 1789
 B. 1791
 C. 1798
 D. 1803

17. _____ said that "the Constitution is whatever the judges say it is..."
 A. James Madison
 B. John Marshall
 C. Charles Evans Hughes
 D. Thurgood Marshall

18. Women obtained the right to vote in the United States in _____.
 A. 1824
 B. 1870
 C. 1920
 D. 1945

19. What happened in 1972?
 A. Congress passed the Equal Rights Amendment, and sent it to the states for ratification.
 B. *Roe v. Wade* was decided by the U.S. Supreme Court.
 C. The Supreme Court upheld the doctrine of romantic paternalism.
 D. The Equal Rights Amendment was added to the U.S. Constitution.

20. Which of the following statements is TRUE?
 A. Most state referendums that impose term limits on members of Congress have failed.
 B. The U.S. Supreme Court has upheld state referendums imposing term limits on members of Congress.
 C. The U.S. Supreme Court has invalidated state referendums imposing term limits on members of Congress.
 D. The U.S. Supreme Court has refused to hear any cases on the constitutionality of term limits on members of Congress.

21. Explain how American constitutionalism predates the British philosopher John Locke.

22. Why was the confederal government created by the Articles of Confederation ineffectual? Explain.

23. What are the major principles of the U.S. Constitution? Be sure to explain each one.

24. How can the U.S. Constitution be changed? Explain.

25. Have women's rights been advanced since the defeat of the Equal Rights Amendment? Explain.

V. Critical Thinking Exercises

1. Do you believe in a literal interpretation of the U.S. Constitution or do you view the document as a living entity that should be applied to contemporary society? Explain using concrete illustrations.

2. Compare and contrast relative strengths and weaknesses of unitary, federal, and confederal systems of government. How does the federal system in the United States affect diversity and hyperpluralism?

VI. Answers to the Practice Exam

1.	C	11.	B
2.	A	12.	B
3.	B	13.	C
4.	B	14.	D
5.	D	15.	A
6.	A	16.	B
7.	C	17.	C
8.	D	18.	C
9.	B	19.	A
10.	A	20.	C

21. American constitutionalism predates John Locke in a number of ways. 400 years before Locke, members of the British nobility forced King John to sign the Magna Carta (1215). The Magna Carta guaranteed certain rights and began a long process to limit the power of the monarchy. In the 1300s, the British Parliament extended these rights to all citizens and institutionalized certain procedural safeguards such as due process. When the British settled Jamestown in 1607, they started a representative assembly under a charter granted by the king. In 1620, the Pilgrims drafted the Mayflower Compact before they even landed in Plymouth. The agreement established a legislative body to create laws for the public good. Other colonial charters established between 1630 and 1732 furthered the idea of limited government.

22. The Articles of Confederation were ratified by the states in 1781 and created a very weak central government. The only branch at the national level of government was a unicameral legislature. There was no executive branch for administrative purposes, and no judiciary to resolve interstate disputes. Each state possessed one vote in the Continental Congress, so Rhode Island had as much political power as Massachusetts. Congressional delegates were selected and compensated by state legislatures, so they were truly beholden to them. While the Congress did have the power to make peace, wage war, coin money, and deal with the Native American tribes, it had no authority to regulate commerce and no power to tax. As a result, chaos reigned, war debts could not be paid, and Continental dollars were virtually worthless. The Continental Congress could not bring order; it had the power to raise an army but no power to fund it.

After the states refused to send the necessary funds, the Continental Congress was forced to disband the army. Due to money problems of their own, many states could not finance state militias either.

23. The core principles of the U.S. Constitution are popular sovereignty, rule of law, republicanism, federalism, separation of powers, checks and balances, and individual rights. Popular sovereignty basically means rule by the people. At the national level, this entails electing officials to rule on behalf of the people. Below the national level, this may involve direct participation by the people in governing (e.g., New England town meetings). The rule of law refers to the notion that citizens and leaders cannot do whatever they desire–they are constrained by written principles and procedures we call law. The Framers also embraced a belief in republicanism, a form of government where the people are the ultimate sovereigns. Furthermore, they believed that a federal system of government was preferable to the other two extremes (confederal and unitary). In the United States, power and authority is shared between the national government and the states. To the Framers, this would reduce the likelihood of governmental intrusion into basic rights. In addition, they established separation of powers and checks and balances, so no one branch would exceed its constitutional mandate. Lastly, the federalists promised to amend the Constitution after ratification with a formal statement in preservation of individual rights. They fulfilled this when the Bill of Rights was ratified in 1791.

24. The U.S. Constitution can be changed in a number of ways. The first is straightforward: by a formal amendment. This is a two-step process: proposal and ratification. In most cases historically, a proposal requires a two-thirds vote by both houses of Congress. Ratification typically involves approval by three-fourths of the state legislatures, or thirty-eight votes. It is very difficult to garner such supermajorities, and this is why the Constitution has only been amended twenty-seven times in history. Besides a formal amendment, the Constitution can be changed by judicial interpretation. In essence, the U.S. Supreme Court has "amended" the Constitution through its decisions. Fundamental changes in American culture have also directly and indirectly affected the Constitution and how the courts interpret it. New eras foster new questions and place different demands on the Constitution.

25. Despite the defeat of the Equal Rights Amendment, women's rights have been advanced due to judicial interpretation. In 1973, for example, the Supreme Court ruled that the military must provide the same benefits for its members regardless of gender. In the majority opinion, Justice William Brennan examined the history of gender discrimination rationalized by romantic paternalism. In *Roe v. Wade*, the justices extended the rights of women by ruling that the right to privacy includes the right to have an abortion, at least in the first trimester. Women's rights have also been expanded by legislative action. Affirmative action programs, for example, have benefitted many women by expanding their opportunities in the workforce.

CHAPTER 3
AMERICAN POLITICAL DEVELOPMENT

I.   Summary

The author examines growth and change in the American political experience by focusing on four recurring trends in America's political development: unity, democratization, modernization, and prosperity. Two concepts used to study politics, political culture and political development, assist students in understanding why the American political system is fraught with diversity and hyperpluralism. During the quest for unity, central authority was established but encouraged diversity in the long term because ultimate power was given to the people. The pursuit of democratic ideals has also promoted hyperpluralism. Democratization has historically entailed extending the ideals and practices of participation to an ever larger proportion of the population. In America, this has been witnessed by the extension of voting rights and making democratic processes more accessible to ordinary citizens. Modernization has also advanced hyperpluralism because government has gradually taken a more active role in protecting workers and regulating industries. In turn, this has encouraged Americans to think of themselves of members of particular groups. Lastly, in the search for prosperity, a governmental commitment to the well-being of ordinary citizens truly began with the New Deal in the 1930s and is deeply entrenched in American politics in the form of many popular programs. In a sense, the search for prosperity in the United States has furthered the trend toward diversity by elevating people's expectations of the federal government.

II.   Outline

III.   Key Terms, Concepts, Events, and People

Be able to identify and/or define each of the following and state its importance in a short paragraph.

Political culture (p.55)

Mass political subculture (p.55)

Elite political subculture (p.56)

Traditionalistic political subculture (p.56)

Moralistic political subculture (p.56)

Individualistic political subculture (p.56)

Political development (p.57)

Unification stage (p.58)

Modernization stage (p.58)

Welfare stage (p.58)

Abundance stage (p.58)

Northwest Ordinance (1787) (p.59)

American exceptionalism (p.61)

Manifest destiny (p.61)

Democratization (p.62)

Suffrage (p.62)

Suffragettes (p.62)

Progressivism (p.64)

Australian or secret ballot (p.64)

Split-ticket voting (p.64)

Initiative (p.64)

Referendum (p.64)

Recall (p.64)

National Voter Registration Act (1993) (p.64)

Civil service (p.67)

Workers' compensation (p.68)

Federal income tax (p.68)

22

Labor unions (p.68)

New Deal (p.69)

Social Security Act of 1935 (p.69)

Securities Exchange Act (p.69)

Federal Deposit Insurance Corporation(p.69)

Cold War (p.70)

Guns and butter (p.71)

Postindustrial (p.71)

IV.   Practice Exam

(Answers appear at the end of this chapter)

1. Which of the following is part of the elite political subculture?
   A. Ordinary Americans
   B. President
   C. Federal judges
   D. Both b + c

2. Which of the following states is an example of a predominantly traditionalistic political subculture?
   A. Minnesota
   B. Washington
   C. Mississippi
   D. New York

3. Which of the following states is an example of a predominantly moralistic political subculture?
   A. Louisiana
   B. Texas
   C. Maine
   D. Alaska

4. Which of the following states is an example of a predominantly individualistic political subculture?
   A. Indiana
   B. Georgia
   C. New Hampshire
   D. Alabama

5. _____ argued that the Articles of Confederation were "a national humiliation."
   A. Alexander Hamilton
   B. Thomas Jefferson
   C. George Mason
   D. John Marshall

6. What happened as a result of the French and Indian Wars?
   A. Spain controlled all of North America east of the Mississippi River.
   B. France controlled all of North America east of the Mississippi River.
   C. Great Britain controlled all of North America east of the Mississippi River.
   D. Great Britain made a huge profit.

7. The Louisiana Purchase was made in _____ and was sold by _____.
   A. 1781, Spain
   B. 1790, Great Britain
   C. 1803, France
   D. 1837, Russia

8. Congress purchased Alaska from _____ in _____.
   A. Russia, 1867
   B. Russia, 1959
   C. Germany, 1911
   D. China, 1889

9. In 1898, the United States declared war on _____.
   A. China
   B. Spain
   C. Germany
   D. Russia

10. Black males obtained the right to vote constitutionally in _____.
    A. 1845
    B. 1870
    C. 1920
    D. 1945

11. Poll taxes were eliminated
    A. by a congressional statute.
    B. by a constitutional amendment.
    C. by the U.S. Supreme Court.
    D. by administrative decree.

12. Women obtained the vote nationally in the United States in _____.
    A. 1848
    B. 1887
    C. 1920
    D. 1952

13. What was the impact of some of the changes made in American political processes during the Progressive Era?
    A. Political corruption increased.
    B. The political process was democratized.
    C. Political parties were weakened.
    D. Both b + c.

14. Progressives thought that government could be made more efficient
    A. through the spoils system.
    B. through powerful political parties.
    C. through exploiting the voters.
    D. through a professional civil service.

15. The federal income tax
    A. was adopted by President Herbert Hoover during the Great Depression.
    B. was adopted by President Franklin Roosevelt during the New Deal.
    C. was adopted by a constitutional amendment in 1791.
    D. was adopted by a constitutional amendment in 1913.

16. What was the New Deal?
    A. It was a package of federal programs designed to stimulate economic recovery.
    B. It was a package of federal programs advocated by President Herbert Hoover.
    C. It was a package of federal programs advocated by President Woodrow Wilson.
    D. It was a package of federal programs designed to enhance the nuclear capability of the United States.

17. _____ initiated the War on Poverty.
    A. President Harry Truman
    B. President Lyndon Johnson
    C. President John Kennedy
    D. President Jimmy Carter

18. What has occurred in the 1980s and 1990s?
    A. The incomes of the wealthiest Americans sharply increased.
    B. The poor got poorer.
    C. Both a + b.
    D. The middle class expanded and got richer.

19. Which of the following statements is TRUE?
    A. Most Americans trust the federal government.
    B. Many middle class voters are increasingly frustrated, and often blame political incumbents regardless of party affiliation for their economic stress.
    C. Most Americans are satisfied with either the Republican or Democratic parties.
    D. White males tend to support diversity more so than women and African Americans.

20. Which of the following statements is TRUE?
    A. Whites tend to be more supportive of affirmative action than African Americans.
    B. African Americans tend to be more supportive of affirmative action than whites.
    C. African Americans and whites tend to have similar opinions on affirmative action.
    D. Whites tend to be more supportive of aid to minorities than African Americans.

21. What are the three distinct political subcultures identified by Daniel Elazar? Be sure to define each, and ascertain where they tend to be predominant.

22. How was a national political ideology developed in the United States? Explain.

23. Explain how voting rights have been extended in U.S. history.

24. How has modernization contributed to America's political development? Explain.

25. What was the New Deal? How did it differ from the status quo? Explain.

V.   Critical Thinking Exercises

1. How could Americans do a better job of contending with diversity in the United States? What role, if any, should the federal government play in promoting diversity? Explain.

2. Trace the history of your own state. Upon doing so, provide an assessment of Daniel Elazar's political subcultures. Did you find his typology compelling? Why or why not?

VI.   Answers to the Practice Exam

1.	D	11.	B
2.	C	12.	C
3.	C	13.	D
4.	A	14.	D
5.	A	15.	D
6.	C	16.	A
7.	C	17.	B
8.	A	18.	C
9.	B	19.	B
10.	B	20.	B

21. The three distinct political subcultures are moralistic, individualistic, and traditionalistic. The moralistic political subculture stresses a public-spirited citizenry dedicated to promoting the greater public good. Widespread political participation is expected and valued. In this type of a culture, politics is viewed positively, as is government intervention in both the economy and society. This subculture tends to be predominant in New England, the upper Midwest, and the Pacific Coast. The individualistic political subculture emphasizes the goals, aspirations, and initiatives of private individuals or groups. Government exists to serve and facilitate these interests, not necessarily to promote the general good. This culture tends to be predominant in the industrial Midwest. The traditionalistic political subculture is characterized by the political dominance of a small elite. Its goal is to maintain the established social and economic order; political participation is typically lowest (of the three) in this type of culture. It is predominant in the South.

22. From the very beginning, Americans of all social classes and backgrounds have valued individual liberty and freedom, political equality, and a balance between majority rule and minority rights. This "American creed" has obviously been flawed in practice, but it has provided ideals that Americans have always universally shared. This creed has given American citizens and leaders the perception that America is uniquely special compared to other nations; this view is known as American exceptionalism. This

ideology fueled the belief that America had a manifest destiny to expand as a nation, which started early in the history of the republic with the Louisiana Purchase in 1803.

23. The U.S. Constitution stipulated that states would run elections in the United States, and thus would determine who would vote. At the founding, this meant that only white males with property had voting rights. In the late 1700s and early 1800s, working class people pressured the states to eliminate property requirements. By the mid-1800s, all states eliminated this stipulation. After the Civil War ended in 1865, the Fifteenth Amendment extended suffrage to the newly freed male slaves, though southern states found many ways to effectively preclude black males from voting (e.g., overt violence, literacy tests, poll taxes, and the white primary). After about a seventy-year struggle, women obtained the right to vote in 1920 with the passage of the Nineteenth Amendment. Later, during the Vietnam War, the voting age was lowered to eighteen (from twenty-one).

24. Modernization has contributed to America's political development in three ways: by pressuring the government to protect both workers and industry, by redefining group identities, and by creating an administrative state. The Industrial Revolution created two contradictory pressures on government: to protect workers from the effects of industrialization and to protect industrialists from the effects of government regulation. To this day, this tenuous balance has been the source of a great deal of political conflict, as Americans continue to demand government services and to support more deregulation simultaneously. A second impact of the modernization era is the way Americans perceive themselves. Historically, Americans have viewed themselves both as individuals and as members of groups. But after the Industrial Revolution, different identities led to different associations. In response to government's increased role in American life, these groups grew in number tremendously, leading to the presence of hyperpluralism. Lastly, prior to modernization, government was greatly limited in size and scope. The Industrial Revolution and the reforms by the Progressives changed this forever. Urban poverty and worker exploitation led to more demands for government intervention. Furthermore, the Progressives believed that government could be made more efficient through a professional civil service. With the New Deal programs of the 1930s and the Great Society programs of the 1960s, the bureaucratic state grew in response to a flurry of legislation designed to improve the lives of American citizens.

25. Herbert Hoover was president when the Stock Market crashed in 1929. He believed that the marketplace would right itself, and that Americans simply needed to be patient. This view epitomized the status quo; at that time the federal government was very small and most believed that it could not do much to revive the economy. Franklin Roosevelt had a much different view of government intervention in the domestic economy. His New Deal was a series of federal programs designed to stimulate economic recovery, assist Depression victims, guarantee minimum living standards, and prevent future economic calamities. Included in Roosevelt's package was the National Recovery Administration, the Agricultural Adjustment Administration, the Public Works Administration, and the Works Progress Administration. The most profound legacy of the New Deal was the Social Security Act of 1935. This is currently the nation's largest and most popular entitlement program. Other New Deal reforms addressed how people invested their money (e.g., the Securities Exchange Act and the Federal Deposit Insurance Corporation) so that individual savers would be protected and public confidence would be enhanced in their financial institutions.

CHAPTER 4
FEDERALISM AND SUBNATIONAL DIVERSITY

I. Summary

Federalism in America is a very complex topic as Americans tend to be philosophical subnationalists on the one hand and operational nationalists on the other because while Americans believe that the federal government has too much power, they also tend to support federal programs already in place and oppose cuts in many of them. American federalism contributes greatly to the politics of diversity. A great deal of variance exists in the implementation of public policies because many federal powers have been devolved back to the states and local governments. As such, there are fascinating contrasts among states and local governments in terms of what they choose to do and spend. The policies enacted reflect the differences between citizens in various regions of the country. The federal structure of the U.S. government also makes hyperpluralism possible. There are more than 85,000 governments in the United States, yet many of these do not work very effectively and fairly for all people. As a result, interest group politics has become increasingly magnified in the United States.

II. Outline

III. Key Terms, Concepts, Events, and People

Be able to identify and/or define each of the following and state its importance in a short paragraph.

Crime Control Act of 1994 (p.80)

Subnational governments (p.81)

Federalism (p.81)

Unitary systems (p.82)

Confederal systems (p.82)

Delegated or enumerated powers (p.84)

Reserved powers (p.85)

Concurrent powers (p.85)

Full faith and credit clause (p.85)

Privileges and immunities (p.85)

Extradition (p.85)

Townships (p.88)

Counties (p.88)

Cities (p.88)

Standard Metropolitan Statistical Areas (SMSAs) (p.88)

Special districts (p.88)

School districts (p.88)

Councils of government (p.88)

Homeowners associations (p.88)

Edge cities (p.89)

Dual federalism (p.89)

McCulloch v. Maryland (1819) (p.89)

Cooperative federalism (p.90)

Picket-fence federalism (p.91)

Centralized federalism (p.91)

Matching funds (p.91)

Crosscutting requirements (p.91)

Crossover sanctions (p.91)

Revenue sharing (p.91)

Preemptions (p.94)

Partial preemptions (p.94)

Mandates (p.94)

Unfunded mandates (p.94)

Developmental policies (p.94)

Redistributive policies (p.94)

Issue networks (p.96)

U.S. Term Limits v. Thornton (1995) (p.98)

IV.   Practice Exam

(Answers appear at the end of this chapter)

Multiple Choice

1.   Which of the following has a federal system of government?
   A.   Canada
   B.   Germany
   C.   Both a + b
   D.   Japan

2.   Which of the following has a unitary system of government?
   A.   France
   B.   Australia
   C.   Mexico
   D.   United Nations

3.   Which of the following statements is TRUE about the U.S. Constitution?
   A.   State governments are not mentioned.
   B.   The District of Columbia is not mentioned.
   C.   Local governments are not mentioned.
   D.   The federal government is not mentioned.

4.   Congress was given a general grant of power in the Constitution under the
   A.   reserved powers clause.
   B.   full faith and credit clause.
   C.   privileges and immunities clause.
   D.   necessary and proper clause.

5.   Which of the following category of governments is largest in the United States?
   A.   Counties
   B.   Municipalities
   C.   Townships
   D.   Special districts

6.   Counties represent a local government idea borrowed from _____.
   A.   France
   B.   Great Britain
   C.   The Netherlands
   D.   Germany

7.   Which of the following statements is TRUE about school districts in the United States?
   A.   They are a form of special districts.
   B.   The number of school districts has been shrinking in the last half-century.
   C.   Both a + b.
   D.   The number of school districts has been increasing in the last half-century.

8.   Which of the following is TRUE about the Supreme Court's decision in *McCulloch v. Maryland*?
   A.   The Court ruled in favor of Maryland.
   B.   The Court invalidated the national banking system established by Congress.
   C.   The Court ruled that federal power is supreme over the states.
   D.   The Court ruled that the necessary and proper clause did not apply to the case.

9.   _____ was a vocal proponent of state-centered federalism.
   A.   John C. Calhoun
   B.   Alexander Hamilton
   C.   John Marshall
   D.   James McCulloch

10. _____ was a watershed event in cooperative federalism.
    A. World War I
    B. The New Deal
    C. The Industrial Revolution
    D. Immigration

11. Which metaphor describes dual federalism?
    A. Texas sheet cake
    B. Layer cake
    C. Marble cake
    D. German chocolate cake

12. _____ persuaded Congress to enact revenue sharing.
    A. President John Kennedy
    B. President Lyndon Johnson
    C. President Richard Nixon
    D. President Gerald Ford

13. Which of the following pairs had similar views about federalism?
    A. Ronald Reagan and Richard Nixon
    B. Ronald Reagan and Lyndon Johnson
    C. Ronald Reagan and Franklin Roosevelt
    D. Ronald Reagan and John Kennedy

14. What is the ultimate block grant program?
    A. A categorical grant.
    B. An unfunded mandate.
    C. A preemption.
    D. Revenue sharing

15. Which of the following is NOT a redistributive policy?
    A. Social Security
    B. Medicare
    C. Aid to Families with Dependent Children
    D. Mass transit systems

16. Which of the following statements is TRUE about poor people today?
    A. Aid for the poor depends on what they need.
    B. Aid for the poor depends on where they live.
    C. Aid for the poor is exclusively a federal issue.
    D. Aid for the poor is exclusively a state issue.

17. Which of the following is a component of the Personal Responsibility and World Opportunity Act?
    A. Welfare was centralized at the federal level.
    B. Time limits were established for those receiving welfare.
    C. Welfare grants to the states were consolidated into categorical grants.
    D. Federal welfare spending doubled.

18. Which of the following trends has occurred over the last few decades?
    A. Subnational governments no longer lobby members of Congress.
    B. Private businesses only lobby members of Congress, not state legislators.
    C. Many states, cities, and counties hire private lobbyists to work on their behalf.
    D. Groups like the U.S. Conference of Mayors and the National Governors Conference no longer function.

19. American views of federalism
    A. tend to be very consistent.
    B. tend to be very inconsistent.
    C. tend to favor a more powerful federal government.
    D. tend to favor a confederal form of government.

20.   In *U.S. Term Limits v. Thornton*, the
        Supreme Court ruled
        A.   that states had the right to limit the
                terms of members of Congress.
        B.   that states did not have the right to
                limit the terms of members of
                Congress.
        C.   that states could limit the terms of
                members of Congress to 12 years.
        D.   that states could only limit the
                terms of local officials.

Essays

21.   How does American federalism include both vertical and horizontal relationships? Explain.

22.   Describe the basic structure of local governments in the United States.

23.   Explain the differences between dual and cooperative federalism.

24.   Carefully explain why certain politicians tend to favor categorical grants, whereas others tend to favor
        block grants.

25.   What three patterns of behavior have emerged in the current era of American federalism? Explain.

V.   Critical Thinking Exercises

1.   What is your opinion of term limits for legislators at both the state and federal levels? Are term limits
        constitutional? Try to develop several justifications in support of your perspective.

2.   How well do you know the subnational geography of the United States? Obtain a blank map of the United
        States (with only the state boundaries included). Try to locate all fifty states (50 points) and simply
        identify each state capital (50 points). Based on a total of 100 points, how well did you do?

VI.   Answers to the Practice Exam

1.	C	11.	B
2.	A	12.	C
3.	C	13.	A
4.	D	14.	D
5.	D	15.	D
6.	B	16.	B
7.	C	17.	B
8.	C	18.	C
9.	A	19.	B
10.	B	20.	B

21.   Vertical relationships involve those between the national government and the subnational (state and local)
        governments. Specific powers were assigned to the federal government under Article I, Section 8 of the

Constitution (e.g., power to wage wars, regulate interstate commerce, raise and spend taxes). Following the enumerated powers, a very broad power to make all laws that are necessary and proper is also included in Article I, Section 8. After these references to federal power, vague references are made to the states (reserved powers under the Tenth Amendment and concurrent powers to promote the general welfare). Horizontal relationships pertain to dealings between the several states. The Constitution includes three such provisions: the full faith and credit clause, to protect citizens' legal rights in civil matters from state to state; privileges and immunities, so citizens from one state traveling to another will enjoy the same rights as residents; and extradition, so if a person is charged with a crime in one state and leaves, he or she can be delivered back to that state to stand trial.

22. Below the state level, there is a great deal of diversity of local governments with an array of governing options. Most states (except for Connecticut or Rhode Island) have counties (in Louisiana they are called parishes, and in Alaska boroughs). Counties are subdivisions of the states and provide a broad array of local services including police protection, road maintenance and construction, and land-use planning. They are administrative arms of the states, and manage state courts, prosecute crimes, administer welfare programs and a host of other activities. Counties raise revenues through a portion of state sales and local property taxes plus user fees. Sixteen states have townships, which are geographical and political subdivisions of counties. Townships carry out county functions such as road maintenance. Cities are municipal corporations. They provide a range of local services including fire and police protection, recreation, and trash collection. Financially, cities rely on their share of sales and property taxes, federal and state aid, and a wide range of fees. Special districts usually provide a single service other local governments cannot or will not provide (e.g., sanitation, transit and street lighting, flood control). Funding comes from property taxes, bonds, and fees tied to the service provided. School districts are a form of special districts. Typically, school districts receive their revenue local property taxes, state aid, and various fees.

23. Dual federalism, or the layer cake metaphor, essentially was an idea that the national and state governments had separate spheres of authority, and did not work together. Dual federalism was a dominant idea in the United States from the founding until the early part of the twentieth century. The national government basically limited itself to specific activities delineated in the Constitution: national defense, foreign affairs, coining money, and powers enumerated in Article I, Section 8. The states made policy on domestic matters such as education, welfare, health, and law enforcement. In actual practice, most governmental activity occurred at the subnational level. As American society became more complex and the Industrial Revolution produced a national economy, the division of labor between the federal and state levels blurred. From the early 1900s to 1964, a pattern of cooperative federalism emerged, or the marble cake metaphor. This refers to a sharing of policy responsibility between federal and state governments, where the federal government was supreme. Franklin Roosevelt's New Deal was the watershed event in cooperative federalism. Cooperative federalism suggested a dependency relationship: states were dependent on the federal government for much-needed grants-in-aid.

24. Categorical grants are a type of grant-in-aid for specific categories of activities. Liberals tend to favor this approach because they believe that some states need to be induced to address certain problems that they might otherwise ignore. Block grants are a type of grant-in-aid where broad grants for generally prescribed activities such as economic development. Block grants are popular with state and local officials because they have relatively few strings attached and officials have a great deal of spending discretion. Conservatives tend to favor this approach because it decentralizes political power from Washington, D.C. to the state and local governments.

25. Three patterns of behavior have emerged in contemporary American federalism. First, subnational governments have become forced to lobby or influence policies made at the federal level. In this competitive environment for resources, many states, cities, and counties, and special districts have

maintained offices in Washington, D.C. and/or hired private lobbyists to work on their behalf. Second, public officials at all levels of government are behaving as policy shifters. Different levels of government are constantly seeking ways to address major problems on an issue by issue basis. The result is an ebb and flow of national and subnational power. Third, citizens are behaving as policy shoppers. They shop for the most responsive level of government, not necessarily the most effective or appropriate. Most Americans have a rather inconsistent view of federalism. Philosophically, most are subnationalists who believe that the federal government is too powerful and obtrusive. Operationally, they are nationalists who support federal programs such as Social Security and Medicare and oppose any cuts in existing benefit levels.

CHAPTER 5
PUBLIC OPINION AND IDEOLOGY

I. Summary

Public opinion in the United States is a very diverse entity. While some suggest that Americans are typically moderate in their views, it is oftentimes difficult to discern public opinion because there are in reality many publics holding many opinions on policy issues. On some subjects, Americans have achieved a consensus (e.g., most Americans agree with the nation's core values of freedom and equality). Yet on other topics, the results of scientific polls suggest that Americans hold a variety of preferences on a multitude of issues. Americans develop their opinions through the process of political socialization, which involves many factors. The role of family is instrumental in the development of political attitudes and political party preferences. Yet other factors, such as schooling, peers, media influence, religion, and life experience, are influential as well. America's diversity is evident when examining the differences between groups, especially race and ethnicity, gender, religion, age, region, and social class. The most profound disagreements between and among Americans typically stem from racial or ethnic identity.

II. Outline

Public Opinion in Action: The Verdict (p.105)
Introduction: Opinion, Ideology, and the Politics of Diversity (p.106)
Public Opinion as Participation (p.108)
 The Knowledge Gap (p.108)
 The Nature of Public Opinion (p.110)
 The Shape of Public Opinion (p.111)
Political Socialization: How Opinions are Formed (p.111)
 Family (p.111)
 School (p.112)
 Peers (p.112)
 Media (p.113)
 Religion (p.113)
 Life Experience (p.114)
Measuring Public Opinion (p.115)
 Straw Polls (p.115)
 Scientific Polling (p.115)
How Polls are Used and Abused (p.116)
Why Americans Disagree: Sources of Diversity (p.118)
 Race and Ethnicity (p.118)
 Gender Differences (p.120)
 Religious Faith (p.120)
 Age Gaps (p.121)
 Social Class (p.122)
 Regional Contrasts (p.122)
Ideology: Diverse Visions of the Good Society (p.123)
 Liberalism and Conservatism (p.123)

III.　Key Terms, Concepts, Events, and People

Be able to identify and/or define each of the following and state its importance in a short paragraph.

Public opinion (p.107)

Beliefs (p.107)

Values (p.107)

Ideology (p.107)

Ideologues (p.107)

Consensus opinion pattern (p.111)

Divisive opinion pattern (p.111)

Mixed opinion pattern (p.111)

Permissive opinion pattern (p.111)

Political socialization (p.111)

Cross-cutting cleavages (p.114)

Straw polls (p.115)

Scientific polling (p.115)

Sample (p.115)

Random sampling (p.115)

Random-digit-dialing (p.115)

Sampling error (p.116)

Benchmark polls (p.116)

Tracking polls (p.116)

Gender gap (p.120)

Social class (p.122)

Liberalism (p.123)

Conservatism (p.123)

Socialists (p.126)

Fascists (p.126)

Libertarianism (p.126)

Centrists (p.126)

Populism (p.126)

IV.   Practice Exam

(Answers appear at the end of this chapter)

Multiple Choice

1.   Scientific public opinion polls illustrate that
    A.   most Americans know who represents them in the U.S. House.
    B.   about eighty percent of Americans can identify the Speaker of the U.S. House.
    C.   about seventy-five percent know the political party affiliation of their representative in the U.S. House.
    D.   Americans know shockingly little about their own political system.

2.   Which of the following statements is an accurate description of the American electorate?
    A.   Many Americans are uninformed about the fundamentals of their own political system.
    B.   Most Americans are disinterested in public affairs.
    C.   Most Americans pay a great deal of attention to public affairs.
    D.   Both a + b.

3.   When asked which political party is more influenced by special interests and lobbyists, American public opinion demonstrates a
    A.   consensus opinion pattern.
    B.   mixed opinion pattern.
    C.   permissive opinion pattern.
    D.   divisive opinion pattern.

4.   When does the process of political socialization begin?
    A.   Early in life, and stops around the age of 12.
    B.   Early in life, and continues into adulthood.
    C.   During high school.
    D.   During college.

5.   Political scientists believe that _____ is the most important factor in political socialization.
    A.   the family
    B.   religion
    C.   the media
    D.   schooling

6.   One study suggested that _____ percent of young people identified with the same political party of their parents.
    A.   12
    B.   33
    C.   59
    D.   84

7. Which of the following statements is TRUE?
   A. High school students tend to be more liberal than college students.
   B. The general public tends to be more liberal than college students.
   C. College students tend to be more liberal than the general public.
   D. Students at less selective colleges tend to be more liberal than students at highly selective schools.

8. Most Americans get their primary news from
   A. the Internet.
   B. newspapers.
   C. weekly magazines.
   D. television.

9. Compared to citizens in other industrialized democracies, Americans
   A. are much more likely to be atheists.
   B. are more religious.
   C. are less religious.
   D. are more likely to be Buddhists.

10. Which of the following statements is TRUE?
    A. Jews tend to be more conservative on social and economic issues than other religious groups.
    B. Catholics tend to be liberal more liberal on social issues than other religious groups.
    C. Protestants all have basically the same view on public policy issues.
    D. White evangelical and fundamentalist churches tend to be more politically conservative than other religious groups.

11. Which group tends to attend church on the most regular basis?
    A. Conservatives
    B. Moderates
    C. Liberals
    D. Ideology has no impact on church attendance.

12. What do we know about straw polls?
    A. The results of straw polls are typically the same as the results of scientific polls.
    B. Straw polls are educated guesses about what the public is thinking.
    C. Straw pollsters rely on unrepresentative samples.
    D. Both b + c.

13. In 1936, the editors of the *Literary Digest* predicted that
    A. Alf Landon would win the presidential election by a landslide.
    B. Franklin Roosevelt would win the presidential election by a landslide.
    C. the presidential election was a dead heat on the eve of Election Day.
    D. Thomas Dewey would defeat Harry Truman for the presidency.

14. What did the editors of the *Literary Digest* do wrong in 1936?
    A. They relied on automobile and telephone registration lists for their survey.
    B. They relied on a random sample of the population for their survey.
    C. They relied exclusively on letters-to the editor.
    D. They focused too much on Democratic voters.

15. Pollsters commonly interview _____ Americans to gauge adult public opinion in the United States.
    A. 450
    B. 1,500
    C. 10,000
    D. 1,000,000

16. Most Gallup polls today
    A. have a margin of error of plus or minus ten percent.
    B. rely on mailed questionnaires.
    C. rely on random-digit-dialing.
    D. rely on face-to-face interviews.

17. Focus groups are used to
    A. gauge public opinion.
    B. manipulate public opinion.
    C. Both a + b.
    D. test the reactions of large groups of citizens to commercials or other political stimuli.

18. Blacks and whites in America
    A. have similar views about racial discrimination.
    B. both oppose many forms of racial segregation and discrimination.
    C. both oppose affirmative action policies.
    D. have similar views about racism and its impact on society.

19. The nation's fastest growing ethnic group is
    A. Caucasian.
    B. Hispanic.
    C. African American.
    D. Asian American.

20. Which of the following statements is TRUE?
    A. Women are more likely to consider themselves to be Republicans than men.
    B. Women are more likely to consider themselves to be Democrats than men.
    C. Women and men do not differ at all when it comes to party affiliation.
    D. Women tend to be more conservative on social policy issues than men.

Essays

21. Should the knowledge gap in American public opinion be a source of concern? Why or why not?

22. When it comes to political socialization, why is it impossible to make steadfast generalizations? Explain.

23. What makes contemporary public opinion polls scientific? Explain.

24. Why does social class tend to lead to disagreement in American politics? Explain.

25. Provide some plausible reasons to explain why political ideologies are inconsistent in American politics.

V.   Critical Thinking Exercises

1. Test your knowledge about contemporary political leaders. Identify the individuals who currently hold the following positions:

    1. Your representative in the U.S. House:
    2. Your two U.S. senators:
    3. Vice president of the U.S.:
    4. U.S. Senate Majority Leader:
    5. U.S. Senate *President Pro Tempore*:
    6. U.S. Senate Minority Leader:
    7. Speaker of the U.S. House:

8. U.S. House Majority Leader:
9. U.S. House Minority Leader:
10. Governor of your state:
11. U.S. Secretary of State:
12. U.S. Secretary of Treasury:
13. U.S. Secretary of Defense:
14. U.S. Attorney General:

2.   Since 1980, there has been a measurable gender gap in presidential elections. What political party does this advantage? Why? Try to illustrate your points with concrete illustrations.

VI.   Answers to the Practice Exam

1.	D	11.	A
2.	D	12.	D
3.	B	13.	A
4.	B	14.	A
5.	A	15.	B
6.	C	16.	C
7.	C	17.	C
8.	D	18.	B
9.	B	19.	B
10.	D	20.	B

21.   Political scientists have not achieved a consensus as to whether or not the knowledge gap in American public opinion should be a source of concern. To some, in a pluralistic or hyperpluralistic democracy, there are numerous attentive publics which replace the need for an informed general public. Also, there is some evidence that suggests that American citizens often make reasonably good decisions based on relatively low levels of information and knowledge. Others believe that knowledge is equated with political power, and little or no knowledge has political consequences. Some political scientists believe strongly that an uninformed citizenry results in great disparities between who participates in the political process and who does not, how effective their political participation is, and who benefits from public policy. These theorists contend that those with a great deal of knowledge about public affairs not only participate more actively in the political process, but wield more influence over policy makers as well.

22.   Political socialization is a very complex subject, and it is impossible to make steadfast generalizations for at least two important reasons. First, we are all individuals, and as such, we all tend to vary a great deal, even children within the same family. One sibling may be highly political, while another may be highly apolitical. While political scientists believe that the family is the most important factor in the political socialization process, the same parents may affect individuals differently. Second, people are not only affected by just one or two agents in the political socialization process. Indeed, they are affected by a multitude of factors, including family, education, peers, occupation, race, religion, and a host of others. These factors are called cross-cutting cleavages, and they typically direct people in a variety of directions that do not lend themselves to any simplistic generalizations.

23.   Contemporary polls are scientific if they fulfill four important criteria: (1) pollsters must sample the larger population, and routinely pick between 1,000-1,500 Americans to represent the views of millions; (2) they must conduct a random sample in order to give every potential respondent the same chance of being chosen. Such samples represent the opinion of the larger population, with a relatively small margin of error; (3) pollsters must seek to reduce the sampling error. Since no sample can replicate exactly the entire population, pollsters assign a sampling error (typically no larger than plus or minus four percent) to

their results; and (4) pollsters try to ask the right questions. Pollsters must attempt to ask impartial questions so they do not bias the results of their own survey.

24. Social class involves the grouping of people based on three interrelated factors (income, occupation, and education) and typically leads to disagreements in American politics. Poorer people tend to have low incomes because they have low status occupations and low levels of education. The opposite is true of more affluent Americans. Disagreements between the poor and the rich are apparent in public policy and partisan preferences. Lower income people are more likely than higher income people to be Democrats and support government spending on social policy issues such as jobs programs, housing, and medical care. Higher income people are more likely than lower income people to be Republican and oppose government spending to address social policy issues. There are important differences between Americans when simply focusing on level of education. Compared to people with low levels of education, more educated Americans tend to be better informed about public affairs, they are more likely to vote, and they are more willing to participate in politics. They also tend to more tolerant of people who are not like them and more supportive of civil rights and liberties for all Americans.

25. There are several reasons why political ideologies tend to be inconsistent in American politics. First, many Americans do not think in ideological terms and have little understanding of liberalism and conservatism. Second, many Americans identify themselves as moderates. Defining the political center is a difficult task, because many centrists support government activity up to a point that will vary depending on the issue. Third, ideological consistency depends on the issues being discussed. Both contemporary liberals and conservatives are contradictory to a certain extent. Liberals tend to favor governmental intervention in economic issues but not in social issues; conservatives tend to oppose economic intervention but to favor it in social issues. Fourth, the two-party system encourages Democrats and Republicans to attract nonideologues for votes. In the process, they often take policy positions that are inconsistent with their ideological supporters. Fifth, because of hyperpluralism, interest group politics waters down the politics of ideology. Thousands of interest groups encourage policy makers to respond to their specific demands on a case-by-case basis. As a result, many policy makers seek to solve immediate policy problems rather than consistently promote a particular ideology. Sixth, Americans are individualists, and they view the role of government in highly personal and utilitarian terms. As a result, ideological politics tends to be subordinated and people tend to focus on what governmental policy will do for them as individuals as opposed to its impact on the society as a whole.

CHAPTER 6
THE MEDIA

I.　Summary

The news media play an important role in American politics. In a democracy such as the United States, the media are an important link between the people and the policy makers. Without information, the people would not be able to hold public officials accountable whatsoever. While some contend that the media has either an ideological or structural bias, the presence of hyperpluralism in America minimizes the extent to which any single media outlet can bias public opinion. But the news organizations can exert a great deal of power by deciding what is news. Thus the media may not influence how Americans think to any great extent, but it does affect what Americans think about. The media and public officials have both a symbiotic and an adversarial relationship in which both sides use and abuse each other on a regular basis. Over the past several years, the media has become less diverse due to the fact that many media organizations are becoming concentrated in the hands of a shrinking number of corporate owners. Television remains the most important medium in American society as many rely on television virtually exclusively for all of their daily news.

II.　Outline

III.　Key Terms, Concepts, Events, and People

Be able to identify and/or define each of the following and state its importance in a short paragraph.

Linkage institutions (p.134)

Participatory linkage (p.135)

Policy-responsive linkage (p.135)

Clientele linkage (p.135)

Political news (p.136)

Backgrounders (p.138)

Off the record (p.138)

Leaks (p.138)

Trial balloons (p.138)

Adversarial (p.138)

Attack journalism (p.138)

Elite media (p.140)

Mass media (p.140)

Narrowcasting (p.143)

Pack journalism (p.144)

Issue framing (p.144)

Media bias (p.145)

Ideological bias (p.145)

Sound bites (p.148)

Visual bias (p.148)

Libel (p.148)

Doctrine of prior restraint (p.149)

Federal Communications Commission (FCC) (p.149)

Equal time rule (p.149)

Right of rebuttal (p.149)

Fairness doctrine (p.149)

Telecommunications Act of 1996 (p.150)

Communications Decency Act of 1996 (p.150)

IV.   Practice Exam

(Answers appear at the end of this chapter)

Multiple Choice

1. Which of the following is NOT part of the Big Four?
    A.   *The New York Times*
    B.   *The Washington Post*
    C.   *The Los Angeles Times*
    D.   *The Boston Globe*

2. The most prolific leaker in the administration of Lyndon Johnson was believed to be
    A.   Lyndon Johnson himself.
    B.   Vice president Hubert Humphrey.
    C.   Attorney General Robert Kennedy.
    D.   Secretary of Defense Robert MacNamara.

3. What contributed to the downfall of the Federalist Party in 1800?
    A.   The growing disenchantment with President George Washington.
    B.   The growing disenchantment with the Alien and Sedition Acts.
    C.   The growing disenchantment with President Thomas Jefferson.
    D.   The growing disenchantment with negative campaigning.

4. Which of the following is TRUE about the contemporary media?
    A.   There are currently about 800 newspapers in the United States.
    B.   There are currently about 500,000 television stations in the United States.
    C.   Media outlets are increasing in number, but their owners are decreasing in number.
    D.   Media outlets are decreasing in number.

5. About _____ percent of all American households own at least one television set.
    A.   50
    B.   66
    C.   82
    D.   98

6. About _____ percent of all American households own at least one radio.
    A.   33
    B.   50
    C.   66
    D.   99

7. Americans trust _____ more than any other news source.
    A.   the Internet
    B.   television
    C.   radio
    D.   newspapers

8. Older Americans recall listening to the radio to hear President _____ "fireside chats."
    A.   Calvin Coolidge's
    B.   Herbert Hoover's
    C.   Franklin Roosevelt's
    D.   Harry Truman's

9. Television viewers generally did not present contrasting perspectives during
    A.   the Persian Gulf War.
    B.   the Vietnam War.
    C.   the Iranian hostage crisis.
    D.   the O.J. Simpson murder trial.

51

10. _____ once called the media an "effete corps of impudent snobs."
    A. President Ronald Reagan
    B. President John Kennedy
    C. Vice president Spiro Agnew
    D. Vice president Walter Mondale

11. Which of the following is TRUE about the national media?
    A. The national media has a definitive liberal bias.
    B. The national media has a definitive conservative bias.
    C. The national media tends to be negative in its coverage of politicians.
    D. The national media is dominated by people who identify themselves as Republicans.

12. Which of the following is TRUE about today's media?
    A. Today's media allocates more time for political stories than thirty years ago.
    B. Today's media allocates less time for political stories than thirty years ago.
    C. Today's sound bites are shorter than ever before.
    D. Both b + c.

13. _____ prohibits Congress from abridging freedom of the press.
    A. The First Amendment
    B. The Fourteenth Amendment
    C. Public opinion
    D. The freedom of press act of 1789

14. The libel standard in the United States was created in
    A. *New York Times v. Sullivan.*
    B. *New York Times v. U.S.*
    C. *Roe v. Wade.*
    D. *Branzburg v. Hayes.*

15. What did the Supreme Court rule about the Pentagon Papers?
    A. The justices upheld the doctrine of prior restraint.
    B. The justices ruled that the print media can use its own judgment as to when a story is printed.
    C. The justices upheld the government's right to protect national security.
    D. The justices ruled that journalistic freedom is an absolute right.

16. Which of the following statements is TRUE about the media in the United States?
    A. The federal government owns most of the network stations.
    B. The federal government regulates the broadcast media.
    C. The FCC rarely renews the licenses of radio and television stations.
    D. The FCC performance standards are very specific and clear to all networks.

17. Why is the equal time rule more myth than fact?
    A. Because the networks tend to favor Republicans over Democrats.
    B. Because the networks tend to favor Democrats over Republicans.
    C. Because the networks tend to favor extreme candidates over mainstream candidates.
    D. Because television advertising is very expensive.

18. Which of the following is TRUE of media interest group coverage over the last three decades?
    A. The labor unions tend to get most of the coverage.
    B. Corporations and business groups tend to get most of the coverage.
    C. Farmers tend to get most of the coverage.
    D. Citizen action groups tend to get covered in a favorable manner.

19. Almost half of all network nightly news programs about African Americans focus on
    A. professional athletes.
    B. education.
    C. citizen action groups.
    D. crime, politics, and black victimization.

20. The women who are mentioned most positively in newspapers tend to be
    A. entertainers.
    B. political leaders.
    C. candidates for high political office.
    D. middle managers in public bureaucracies.

Essays

21. How can the media either help or hinder social movements? Explain.

22. Explain why although the number of media outlets is enormous, there is a growing concentration of media ownership in the United States. What questions arise from this reality?

23. Describe four ways that the political power of television expresses itself.

24. How is structural bias manifested in the media? Explain.

25. What major axioms or principles govern the print media in the United States? Explain.

V. Critical Thinking Exercises

1. Over a period of one week, develop a detailed list of your news sources (e.g., television, newspapers, periodicals, radio, and the Internet). How much time, approximately, did you devote to each source? Which source(s) did you use most extensively? Upon doing this exercise, what have you learned about your own habits concerning news information?

2. Many believe that journalists tend to be negative in covering politicians in American national government. Watch the evening news (network of your choice) copiously for an extended period of time. Based on your own criteria, did you also find that journalists tend to cover national politicians in an unflattering manner? Explain using concrete illustrations from your study.

VI. Answers to the Practice Exam

1.	D	11.	C
2.	A	12.	D
3.	B	13.	A
4.	C	14.	A
5.	D	15.	B
6.	D	16.	B
7.	B	17.	D
8.	C	18.	B
9.	A	19.	D
10.	C	20.	A

21. The media can help or hinder social movements by paying attention to or ignoring their issues. The media can enhance social movements by providing extensive coverage. For example, television encouraged sympathy for the civil rights movement by airing pictures of police beating black

demonstrators. The opponents to the Vietnam War were benefitted when major networks covered the gory and unflattering aspects of America's military involvement. Media organizations can also grant social movement activists and organizers direct access to the airwaves. If the mainstream media ignores activists, they must develop their own media outlets. The contemporary women's movement has utilized both the mainstream media and the alternative feminist media to advance its agenda. Many social movements who do not get much traditional coverage have developed their own newspapers, newsletters, magazines, and television programs. In addition, any group can develop a home page on the Internet.

22.   The whole number of media outlets in the United States is quite extensive. There are more than 12,000 newspapers, 7,000 radio stations, 1,600 television stations, 11,000 periodicals, and 2,600 book publishers. Yet while outlets are increasing in number, their owners are decreasing in number for many of these outlets are being bought up by media and corporate conglomerates. For example, the Walt Disney Corporation owns multiple production companies, a publishing house, and Capital Cities/ABC which owns ABC television, several cable stations, and the *Kansas City Star*. A growing concentration of media ownership raises serious questions in a democracy. Among them are: will those who produce the news be willing to criticize the corporations that pay their salaries; will those who produce the news be willing to uncover corporate scandals for the corporations that pay their salaries; and will those who produce the news cover the political contributions of the corporations that pay their salaries?

23.   The political power of television expresses itself in numerous ways. First, it helps to frame and prioritize policy issues. Journalists employ both hypothetical and concrete news stories, and in so doing researchers have discovered that the mere coverage of events or issues heightens their importance in the perceptions of viewers. Second, television is powerful because it provides access. In fact, television has allowed many candidates to dispense with door-to-door campaigning and utilize most of their budgets on television advertisements. Without television, contemporary candidates would have a more difficult time packaging their campaigns and creating images to enhance their candidacies. Third, television has the power to "presidentialize" American politics. Television news tends to portray the president as a solitary all-powerful individual, who exerts leadership apart from the other institutions of government. This, of course, puts forth a false image because the president operates in a system of separation of powers and checks and balances. Fourth, television exerts power by affecting how policy makers do their work. For example, presidents can bypass Congress and attempt to manipulate public opinion by appealing directly to the people via a prime time presidential address to the nation. Similarly, members of Congress who oppose the president can do the same thing by appearing on television programs to delineate their views. In addition, since television helps to determine what issues are important to constituents, policy makers tend to focus on those issues.

24.   Structural bias comes in many forms. First, there is a fundamental difference in news values between policy makers, reporters, and publishers and media owners. Policy makers want us to believe their version of the problems we face as well as the solutions they offer. Reporters want us to think about policy problems and develop our own views to those problems and to question the prescriptions created by policy makers. Publishers, executives, and owners want us to spend money by purchasing their newspapers or watching their television programs. They also want us to patronize the advertisers who support those news operations. As a result, they typically seek dramatic news stories involving conflict, disaster, and scandal. Second, it is important to remember that reporters file stories. From their perspective, a story needs to contain a human element. This is why the media tends to focus on personal issues and not the highly technical aspects of public policy. Third, the media tends to treat politics as a sporting event. During campaigns, journalists routinely report who is ahead and who is behind in the polls. They tend to focus more on the horse race itself than on public policy issues. A fourth bias is that reporters tend to cover politics and politicians with a negative tone. Coverage of Congress, for example, tends to emphasize scandal, wrongdoing, controversy, intrigue, and sensationalism, and not concrete policy issues. A fifth and major aspect of structural bias is brevity, or the need for news stories to fit into the constraints

of broadcast or print journalism. This is no wonder, since the typical news broadcast is actually twenty-two minutes in length. Lastly, television exhibits a visual bias that newspapers do not. Stories are told in pictures, and not just words. Visual bias refers to the selection and coverage of stories with pictures or visual criteria in mind.

25.   The print media in the United States operates under two axioms or principles. First, journalists can publish almost anything that they want. While the Constitution does not protect libel (malicious, untruthful, or damaging statements made in writing), libel is most difficult to prove. For public officials to prove libel, they must demonstrate "actual malice" and "reckless disregard" for the truth by the media according to the U.S. Supreme Court in *New York Times v. Sullivan* (1964). In practical terms, proving libel is virtually impossible for public figures. Second, reporters can use their own judgment as to when they print a story. In *New York Times v. U.S.* (1971), the Supreme Court rejected the doctrine of prior restraint. In the opinion of Justice Hugo Black, "[o]nly a free and unrestrained press can effectively expose deception in the government."

CHAPTER 7
POLITICAL PARTIES AND INTEREST GROUPS

I.   Summary

The role that political parties and interest groups play in American politics are assessed in this chapter. Political parties organize to espouse certain policies, elect similar-minded candidates, and to organize the policy agenda of governments at all levels. The American political party system is federal in structure, decentralized in operation, and two-party in nature. The electoral rules make it difficult for third parties to succeed, because elections in America feature single-member legislative districts where the winner takes all. The major parties, Democratic and Republican, have been in existence since before the Civil War. Historically, one party dominated politics until a critical realigning election occurred. But today's political parties are very weak and undisciplined. In contrast to the political parties in the United States, American interest groups have become more numerous and powerful in the past few decades. Interest groups form to influence public policy, and they compete with other groups to do so in the American hyperpluralist system. Interest groups represent a multitude of interests and truly are diverse in nature. Some interest groups are more politically powerful than others, depending on their size, availability of resources, and the nature of their membership. Several federal laws have attempted to regulate interest group behavior and how group leaders spend their money, but have been fairly ineffective on both counts. Modern American politics features a three-way relationship between interest groups, political parties, and candidates for public office.

II.   Outline

III.   Key Terms, Concepts, Events, and People

Be able to identify and/or define each of the following and state its importance in a short paragraph.

Political parties (p.161)

Party platforms (p.161)

Party in the electorate (p.162)

Party organization (p.162)

Party in government (p.162)

Party identification (p.162)

National committee (p.164)

State central committees (p.164)

Political machines (p.164))

Two-party system (p.166)

Broker parties (p.166)

Monoparty systems (p.166)

Multiparty systems (p.166)

Single-member legislative districts (p.167)

Winner-take-all electoral system (p.167)

Proportional representation system (p.167)

Minor parties (p.167)

Missionary parties (p.167)

Party eras (p.167)

Critical election (p.167)

Party realignment (p.167)

Responsible party model (p.172)

Progressivism (p.172)

Direct primary (p.173)

Interest group (p.174)

Dissonance theory (p.175)

Political action committees (Pacs) (p.183)

Segregated fund Pacs (p.183)

Nonconnected political committees (p.183)

Iron triangles (p.184)

Subgovernments (p.184)

Issue networks (p.184)

Astroturf lobbying (p.184)

Federal Regulation of Lobbying Act (1946) (p.186)

Ethics in Government Act (1978) (p.186)

IV.   Practice Exam

(Answers appear at the end of this chapter)

Multiple Choice

1.   Tobacco PACs give the vast majority of their political contributions to
   A.   liberals.
   B.   Democrats.
   C.   Republicans.
   D.   Libertarians.

2.   _____ is largely responsible for the creation of the Reform Party.
   A.   Jesse Jackson
   B.   Jerry Brown
   C.   Jack Kemp
   D.   Ross Perot

3.   How would you describe American political parties?
   A.   They are highly disciplined.
   B.   They are highly centralized in operation.
   C.   They are very weak compared to parties in other democracies.
   D.   They are very strong compared to parties in other democracies.

4.   The last of the great political bosses was
   A.   Richard Daley.
   B.   Federico Pena.
   C.   Raymond Flynn.
   D.   Ed Koch.

5.   Why are there only two major political parties in the United States?
   A.   Because the United States has proportional representation.
   B.   Because the United States has single-member legislative districts.
   C.   Because the United States has a winner-take-all electoral process.
   D.   Both b + c.

6.   _____ organized the Federalist party in the early years of the republic.
   A.   George Washington
   B.   Alexander Hamilton
   C.   Thomas Jefferson
   D.   James Madison

7.   _____ organized the Democratic-Republican party in the early years of the republic.
   A.   John Adams
   B.   Thomas Jefferson
   C.   John Marshall
   D.   James Monroe

8.   _____ organized the Democratic party in the 1820s.
   A.   Abraham Lincoln
   B.   Thomas Jefferson
   C.   Andrew Jackson
   D.   William Henry Harrison

9.   _____ ended the Republican dominance of national politics.
   A.   Slavery
   B.   The Great Depression
   C.   The Whigs
   D.   The Vietnam War

10. Which of the following statements is TRUE?
    A. The Republicans ushered in a new realignment in 1994.
    B. The Democrats ushered in a new realignment in 1996.
    C. Divided government has become the norm in the United States.
    D. The strongest Democratic region in the United States is the South.

11. Massachusetts was founded by _____.
    A. Catholics
    B. Quakers
    C. Methodists
    D. Puritans

12. After the founding period, the first wave of growth in interest groups in the United States occurred
    A. in the 1820s and 1830s.
    B. in the 1880s and 1890s.
    C. in the 1920s and 1930s.
    D. in the 1950s and 1960s.

13. The Grange was organized to protect _____ from the monopolistic practices of big business.
    A. the people
    B. farmers
    C. factory workers
    D. doctors

14. What civil rights organization was founded in 1909?
    A. National Organization for Women
    B. League of United Latin American Citizens
    C. National Association for the Advancement of Colored People
    D. Common Cause

15. The biggest single-issue spenders among interest groups are
    A. business groups.
    B. citizen groups.
    C. environmental groups.
    D. abortion rights groups.

16. Which of the following is NOT part of the iron triangle?
    A. Interest groups
    B. Legislative committees
    C. Courts
    D. Government agencies

17. A record number of *amicus curiae* briefs were filed in _____.
    A. *Reno v. ACLU* (1997)
    B. *Brown v. Board of Education* (1954)
    C. *Webster v. Reproductive Health Services* (1989)
    D. *Buckley v. Valeo* (1976)

18. Lobbying is protected in the United States by
    A. common law.
    B. federal regulations.
    C. the First Amendment.
    D. state regulations.

19. Which law grew out of the Watergate scandal?
    A. Federal Regulation of Lobbying Act
    B. Ethics in Government Act
    C. Lobbying Disclosure Act
    D. Federal Election Campaign Act

20. Which of the following is TRUE about soft money?
    A. The biggest soft money contributors to Republicans were oil, gas, and tobacco interests.
    B. The biggest soft money contributors to Democrats were trial lawyers, organized labor, and the entertainment industry.
    C. Both a + b.
    D. According to federal law, groups can only contribute a maximum of $5,000 to the political party of their choice.

21. Explain why the relationship between political parties and interest groups is symbiotic.

22. Demonstrate why political parties are important to American voters and policy makers alike.

23. Describe the party eras that have occurred in U.S. history.

24. Why are some interest groups more powerful than others? Explain.

25. Besides traditional lobbying, what other strategies are employed to link interest group members to the U.S. political system? Explain.

V.   Critical Thinking Exercises

1. Political scientist Theodore Lowi has suggested that America needs a "responsible three-party system." Assess Lowi's proposal: do you agree with his assertion or not? If you agree, what characteristics would the third-party have? If you disagree, explain why.

2. There has been a great deal of discussion about banning soft money in political campaigns in recent years. Depending upon your position on this issue, present a cogent argument for or against such a proposal.

VI.   Answers to the Practice Exam

1.	C	11.	D
2.	D	12.	A
3.	C	13.	B
4.	A	14.	C
5.	D	15.	A
6.	B	16.	C
7.	B	17.	C
8.	C	18.	C
9.	B	19.	D
10.	C	20.	C

21. The relationship between American political parties and interest groups is symbiotic because both operate in the same political system. A system is a collection of components interacting with each other for a common purpose. While interest groups promote their interests by attempting to influence government, political parties seek to nominate candidates and assume responsibility for the management of government. The U.S. political party system is dominated by two political parties, and seems increasingly ineffective at representing the diverse views of Americans. By contrast, the interest group system in America consists of thousands of different groups and is increasingly effective in giving voice to and even splintering those diverse views. Some contend that interest groups dominate public policy making in the United States, not political parties. Yet the combination of political parties and interest groups is a key feature of American hyperpluralism.

22. Although American political parties are weak, they are still important to voters and policy makers alike. First, political parties provide labels with which people identify. Some labels communicate a consistent philosophy about the proper role of government in society. Other labels communicate a longstanding tradition and history. Second, all political parties have policy preferences they would like to enact as law. Many of these views can be found in party platforms. While they may not always represent the views of

all party supporters, platforms do help to frame voter choices during campaigns and the policy agendas that follow. Third, the most fundamental activity of political parties is to help their candidates get elected–to nominate them and campaign on their behalf. As such, parties help to register voters, raise campaign money, lend campaign expertise, and help to get people to actually vote. Fourth, once elected, policy makers use party platforms to formulate at least some of the government's policy agenda. The partisan structure of Congress is testimony to the role of parties in organizing the government's agenda.

23. The first partisan divisions actually predated the establishment of the American republic in 1789. Following the drafting of the Constitution, the Federalists favored ratification and the Anti-Federalists did not. Following ratification, the presidency of George Washington was nonpartisan, but several members of his administration were highly partisan. From the 1790s to the early 1820s, two political parties emerged. The Federalists were led by Alexander Hamilton, and they advocated a strong national government. The leader of the rival party, the Democratic-Republicans, was Thomas Jefferson, and supporters favored a limited national government and states rights–a view of the Constitution that emphasized the reserved powers of the states at the expense of national power. The Federalists' support came primarily from Northeast commercial interests; the Democratic-Republicans' support came primarily from the South and in rural areas. Following the 1800 national elections, the Democratic-Republicans dominated the national government, and the Federalists gradually died out. The Democrats and Whigs dominated from the 1820s to 1860. Like the Federalists, the Democratic-Republicans experienced internal dissension. One faction that emerged from this dissension was led by Andrew Jackson (Democrats). The Democrats favored strong state government and a limited national government. Jackson succeeded in increasing political participation by ordinary Americans in politics. The opposition party was the Whigs. The Whigs opposed Jackson's agenda and defended the interests of both northern businesses and southern planters. The Whigs subsequently split over the slavery issue, paving the way for the creation of the Republican party of Abraham Lincoln. From 1860 to 1932, the Republicans dominated national politics at the expense of the Democrats. This lengthy period of political dominance truly included two separate eras. The Republican party that dominated from 1860 to 1896 was the party of abolitionism. From 1896 to 1932, the Republican party had evolved into a party presumably in favor of protecting the interests of big business. The next era was the New Deal coalition of the 1930s to 1968. The Great Depression ended the Republican dominance of national politics. Franklin Roosevelt's New Deal coalition included labor unions, urban residents, Southerners, Catholics, Jews, and African Americans. Many programs established during the New Deal and the Great Society benefitted vast numbers of Americans, not simply the poor. Since 1968, divided government has been the norm in the United States. In this era of dealignment, neither major party has dominated over the other in national politics.

24. Some interest groups wield much more power than others. The reasons why can be traced to the resources available to each group. One resource is a group's sheer size. Large interest groups with millions of members (e.g., American Association of Retired Persons and the American Automobile Association) command attention simply because of their numbers. A second resource is the very nature of the group membership. Some groups may lack size but may compensate for it with intensity of belief and cohesiveness of purpose. Ideological groups tend to fit in this category. A third resource is money. Some groups can afford to spend a great deal of money on lobbying and maintain a visible presence in Washington, D.C. Some own their own office buildings and have large staffs, maintain constant public relations efforts, and routinely contribute to political candidates.

25. There are several strategies employed to link interest group members to the U.S. political system besides traditional lobbying. One strategy is the use of public relations– interest groups attempt to manipulate public opinion just like politicians. Another one involves electioneering. Interest groups actively seek to both elect their allies and defeat their enemies. Helping an ally win political office is much easier than persuading an opponent to change his or her political views. The rise of political action committees

(PACs) has allowed interest groups of all shapes and sizes to contribute to legislative campaigns. A third strategy is grassroots lobbying. Interest groups do not simply leave lobbying to the experts. They cannot afford to do so in a representative democracy. As a result, they integrate grassroots efforts to involve their own members and the general public in a political movement. A fourth strategy that has become increasingly common in recent decades is litigation. Interest groups often find that they can use judges to make policies through interpreting the U.S. Constitution, federal statutes, and administrative rulings. In many situations, the most effective method of participation by an interest group is to litigate. Lastly, since there are thousands of interest groups varying in size and strength, working alone sometimes is not plausible. As a result, many groups form coalitions or alliances with other groups and pool their resources in order to gain more influence on the political process.

CHAPTER 8
POLITICAL BEHAVIOR, ELECTIONS, AND CAMPAIGNS

I.   Summary

American political behavior is quite diverse, and this creates dilemmas for elected officials as diverse public opinions give politicians mixed messages and very little direction in making policy. Furthermore, it is a virtual guarantee for all public officials that taking any position on any issue will surely alienate some portion of the electorate. Since politics involves a competition for scarce resources, there are always winners and losers as a result of public policy making. Conflict is thus inherent in the political process. Complicating matters is the reality that the United States is moving toward a politically polarized, two tier society: those who vote and those who do not. Those who tend to vote regularly are white, middle class or above, and older. Politicians tend to be more receptive to the policy demands of voters; reducing services to nonvoters is typically an easy choice for a lot of policymakers. A third issue is the trend that Americans support of devolving their political participation downward to the state and local levels. In a hyperplurastic system, policy debates in Washington, D.C. seem remote and/or irrelevant. In reality, school districts, cities, counties, and states provide most of the services that Americans use on a regular basis. A final trend is that many Americans continue to become politically disengaged. Compared to other Western democracies, American voter turnout rates are low. Some analysts blame the electoral process and the conduct of election campaigns for this state of affairs.

II.   Outline

III.   Key Terms, Concepts, Events, and People

Be able to identify and/or define each of the following and state its importance in a short paragraph.

Political participation (p.195)

Spectators (p.196)

Gladiators (p.196)

Political apathetics (p.196)

Exit option (p.197)

Protest option (p.197)

Civil disobedience (p.197)

Political violence (p.197)

Voting age population (VAP) (p.199)

Electorate (p.199)

Voter turnout (p.199)

Voter Registration Act (Motor-voter law) (1993) (p.200)

Special elections (p.200)

Electoral process (p.203)

Electoral mandates (p.203)

Direct primary (p.204)

Closed primaries (p.204)

Semi-closed primaries (p.204)

Semi-open primaries (p.204)

Blanket primaries (p.204)

Runoff primaries (p.204)

Winner-take-all (p.204)

Proportional representation (p.205)

Subnational elections (p.205)

Buckley v. Valeo (1976) (p.206)

Federal Election Campaign Act of (1972) (p.206)

Coattail effect (p.207)

Invisible primary (p.208)

Primary stage (p.208)

Front-loading (p.209)

National nominating conventions (p.209)

Party platform (p.209)

General election campaign (p.209)

Televised debates (p.210)

Prospective (p.210)

Retrospective (p.210)

70

Electoral coalition (p.210)

Maintaining elections (p.211)

Deviating elections (p.211)

Realigning or critical elections (p.212)

Dealignment (p.212)

Permanent campaign (p.212)

Candidate-centered (p.212)

Technology-driven (p.213)

Paid media (p.213)

Free media (p.213)

Civil societies (p.218)

IV.   Practice Exam

(Answers appear at the end of this chapter)

Multiple Choice

1.   Political protest in the United States
     A.   began during the Civil War.
     B.   began during the 1920s.
     C.   began during the 1960s.
     D.   has always been a part of
           American heritage.

2.   The current total population in the United
     States is about _____.
     A.   198,000,000
     B.   248,000,000
     C.   280,000,000
     D.   345,000,000

3.   The national voting age was lowered from
     21 to 18 in _____.
     A.   1920
     B.   1955
     C.   1971
     D.   1984

4.   _____ has no registration
     requirement at all.
     A.   North Dakota
     B.   Tennessee
     C.   Maine
     D.   Arizona

5.   Which of the following is TRUE about voter
     turnout in 1996?
     A.   It was the highest since 1960.
     B.   Less than 49 percent of adults
           voted.
     C.   More than 57 percent of adults
           voted.
     D.   Turnout was higher than 1992.

6.   Who is responsible for primary elections in
     the United States?
     A.   The abolitionists
     B.   Big business
     C.   The Progressives
     D.   The suffragettes

7.   Runoff primaries typically occur in
     A.   New England.
     B.   the Midwest.
     C.   the Rocky Mountain region.
     D.   the South.

8.   There are _____ members of the U.S.
     House of Representatives.
     A.   270
     B.   390
     C.   435
     D.   560

9. About _____ percent of incumbents in U.S. House races are typically reelected for another term.
   A. 33
   B. 50
   C. 75
   D. 90

10. According to federal law, individuals may contribute no more than _____ per candidate per election.
    A. $1000
    B. $5000
    C. $10,000
    D. $25,000

11. _____ Electoral College votes are required to win the presidency.
    A. 270
    B. 380
    C. 435
    D. 538

12. Which of the following is NOT a constitutional qualification for being president?
    A. 35 years old
    B. Natural born citizen
    C. Member of a political party
    D. U.S. resident for 14 years

13. In 1996, _____ won the New Hampshire primary for the Republicans.
    A. Bob Dole
    B. Pat Buchanan
    C. Lamar Alexander
    D. Steve Forbes

14. For most of the nineteenth century,
    A. presidential candidates typically campaigned from their front porches.
    B. presidential candidates did not actively campaign at all.
    C. presidential candidates typically campaigned via the railroad.
    D. presidential candidates typically campaigned by giving speeches in large cities.

15. When was the last time the U.S. House selected a president?
    A. It has never happened in U.S. history.
    B. 1800
    C. 1824
    D. 1888

16. When was the last time the winner of the popular vote lost the presidency in the Electoral College?
    A. It has never happened in U.S. history.
    B. 1824
    C. 1876
    D. 1888

17. Which of the following does NOT accurately describe contemporary campaigns?
    A. Today's campaigns are party-centered.
    B. Today's campaigns are candidate-centered.
    C. Today's campaigns are technology-driven.
    D. Today's campaigns are permanent in nature.

18. Roughly _____ percent of all U.S. Senate campaigns use television.
    A. 20
    B. 45
    C. 70
    D. 90

19. _____ has twenty percent of the Electoral votes needed to become president.
    A. Texas
    B. Michigan
    C. Pennsylvania
    D. California

20. Negative campaigning
    A. did not occur during Thomas Jefferson's era.
    B. is as old as the republic.
    C. began in the television era.
    D. did not occur during Abraham Lincoln's era.

73

21.   Trace the history of political protest in the United States. Who is likely to engage in protest activities? Explain.

22.   Why are there so many nonvoters in the United States when voting is a cherished right? Explain.

23.   What two fundamental rules govern the presidential election process? Explain.

24.   Besides the requirement of winning a simple majority to get elected, why is the Electoral College an important part of the presidential election process?

25.   How are modern campaigns fundamentally different from those in the nineteenth century?

V.   Critical Thinking Exercises

1.   Ascertain whether or not voting is important to you. Are you registered to vote (citizens in every state except for North Dakota have to voluntarily register themselves)? Do you vote regularly? Why or why not? Does voting make you feel good as a citizen? Can you exercise political power in other ways besides voting? If so, how?

2.   Revisit the discussion of political culture in Chapter 3, and then reflect on the voter turnout by state in the 1992 presidential election in Figure 8.3. What impact does political culture have on voter turnout? Would you expect turnout to be highest in states dominated by a moralistic, individualistic, or traditionalistic political cultures? Explain.

VI.   Answers to the Practice Exam

1.	D	11.	A
2.	C	12.	C
3.	C	13.	B
4.	A	14.	B
5.	B	15.	C
6.	D	16.	D
7.	D	17.	A
8.	C	18.	D
9.	D	19.	D
10.	A	20.	B

21.   Political protest is a nonconventional method of political participation. The idea behind protest is to use it to bring about political or policy change. Political protest has always been a part of America's political heritage dating back to at least 1773 with the Boston Tea Party. Throughout American history, numerous protests have occurred: labor strikes, civil rights marches, and antiwar demonstrations to name a few. Peaceful protests which violate existing laws are considered to be forms of civil disobedience. A very small proportion of Americans are likely to engage in political protest, but one's ethnicity is an important variable. One recent study suggested that nine percent of African Americans had engaged in political protest; and only five percent of whites and 4 percent of Hispanic Americans had done so. The most eloquent spokesperson for peaceful protest was Martin Luther King, Jr.

22.   Researchers believe that there are several reasons why so many Americans do not exercise their right to

vote in spite of the fact that the right to vote is so highly cherished. Among these are election type and frequency, voter indifference, and unclear choices. The level of interest in elections in the United States peaks with presidential elections, and diminishes in state and local elections. In addition, Americans are inundated with elections (e.g., primaries, general elections, special elections, off-year elections, and advisory elections). The high frequency of elections has the cumulative effect of lowering interest and turnout. Voter indifference is high in particular demographical groups, including the poor, the less educated, and the youthful. Younger Americans, for example, tend to find jobs, friends, and leisure activities much more fascinating than public affairs. Political indifference suggests apathy; and apathy suggests passiveness. Yet it is important to remember that some Americans are not simply passive, but feel politically alienated. They believe that their vote is unimportant, and thus have deliberately left the electoral process. Lastly, many elections are not interesting to Americans because many are not very competitive; for a host of reasons, incumbents have distinct advantages over their challengers. The reality of issueless campaigns and the failure of the major parties to provide distinct "cues" to voters also contributes to this phenomenon.

23. The first rule that governs the presidential election process involves the Electoral College, an entity created by the Framers which is directly responsible for electing a president. The Constitution stipulates that an individual needs a simple majority of the Electoral College to become president. Since the Electoral College is a group of 538 people today, the first rule is the number 270. Any candidate who garners 270 Electoral College votes becomes the next president. The second rule involves winning party nominations. The candidate who brings the most pledged delegates to the national convention wins the party's presidential nomination. Thus, the entire presidential election process ultimately comes down to two intense searches–for delegates to get nominated and electoral votes to get elected.

24. Although the Electoral College seems antiquated to many, it remains an important part of the presidential election process for three primary reasons. First, it influences where candidates spend their limited resources. Because seven states (California, New York, Texas, Florida, Pennsylvania, Illinois, and Ohio) provide over three-fourths of the requisite votes to become president, candidates inevitably spend a great deal of time campaigning in these states, especially if they have a reasonable chance of winning. Second, because the Electoral College is a winner-take-all system, it is possible to win the popular vote by a small margin but achieve a landslide in the College. These electoral "landslides" allow presidents to claim a mandate to govern. Third, the Electoral College balances out the exaggerated importance of small, homogeneous states like New Hampshire and Iowa have in the nominating process. In the general election, candidates are forced to address the diverse concerns of the urban and suburban dwellers in the most populous states.

25. Modern political campaigns are different from those of the nineteenth century in at least three fundamental ways. First, today's campaigns, especially those for national office, are constant ongoing affairs. The permanent campaign is party a function of the fact that elections in the United States are regular and predictable. Relatively short, fixed terms (particularly for U.S. House members) encourage the permanent campaign. Second, today's campaigns are no longer run by the political parties. They are candidate-centered. The candidates run their own campaigns–they recruit themselves, establish their own personal organizations, and raise their own campaign money. In the nineteenth century when parties were strong, they were the primary focus of political campaigns, not the candidates. Third, unlike the past, today's campaigns are technology-driven. Modern technology has replaced door-to-door campaigning in many areas. The most dominant technology is television, though computers and the Internet are widely used in campaigns as well.

CHAPTER 9
THE CONGRESS

I.   Summary

The contemporary Congress is more pluralistic than ever, and it contributes to hyperpluralism more than the other two branches. Members of Congress are elected as individuals by states and local districts and go to Washington, D.C. with regional or local viewpoints on public policy issues. Members have always been responsive to organized interests as well, as Congress is the representative branch of government. Law making is the chief function of Congress although budgeting consumes increasing amounts of the members' time. The other broad functions include representation, executive oversight, and civic education. Unlike previous eras in American history, many senators and representatives have become career entrepreneurs who are the leaders of their own political organizations and have become masters of constituent service, the powers of incumbency, election fund raising, and close interest group relationships. The very structure of the national government and the Congress itself promotes political gridlock. In order to conducts its business, Congress is highly fragmented and divided into numerous standing committees and subcommittees. The three branches devised by the Framers of the Constitution also adds to the fragmented political system as both the president and Congress have explicit policy making responsibilities, and the federal courts at times make policy via judicial interpretation. In addition, the conduct of American elections allows for divided government, where the voters may select one political party to control one or more houses of Congress and the other the presidency. This often leads to less congressional productivity and greater interbranch conflict.

II.   Outline

III.   Key Terms, Concepts, Events, and People

Be able to identify and/or define each of the following and state its importance in a short paragraph.

Pork (p.225)

Pork barrel spending (p.225)

Bills (p.228)

Act (p.228)

Joint resolutions (p.228)

Discretionary spending (p.229)

Mandatory spending (p.229)

Budget reconciliation process (p.229)

Appropriation bills (p.229)

Authorization bills (p.229)

Caucuses (p.229)

Casework (p.229)

Home style (p.230)

Trustees (p.230)

Politicos (p.231)

Executive oversight (p.231)

Political oversight (p.231)

Logrolling (p.232)

Standing committees (p.234)

Joint committees (p.234)

Conference committees (p.234)

Select committees (p.234)

Constituency committees (p.234)

Power committees (p.234)

Policy committees (p.235)

Juice committees (p.235)

Party caucuses (p.235)

Personal-interest caucuses (p.235)

Constituency-based caucuses (p.235)

Staff agencies (p.236)

Filibuster (p.237)

Cloture (p.237)

Unanimous consent agreements (p.237)

Veto (p.238)

Pocket veto (p.238)

Line-item veto (p.238)

Third house (p.238)

Gridlock (p.240)

Bicameralism (p.241)

Advise and consent power (p.242)

Reapportionment (p.244)

Powers of incumbency (p.246)

Popular gridlock (p.251)

IV.   Practice Exam

(Answers appear at the end of this chapter)

Multiple Choice

1.   Discretionary spending accounts for _____ percent of the federal budget.
    A.   33
    B.   50
    C.   66
    D.   85

2.   _____ is the fundamental organizing principle of Congress.
    A.   Gender
    B.   Partisanship
    C.   Ethnicity
    D.   Age

3.   What is the second most powerful position in the federal government?
    A.   Vice president
    B.   Senate Majority Leader
    C.   House Speaker
    D.   Chief Justice of the Supreme Court

4.   The day-to-day presiding duties in the U.S. Senate rest with
    A.   the vice president.
    B.   the president *pro tempore*
    C.   junior senators.
    D.   the Chair of the Governmental Affairs committee.

5.   What is the legislative counterpart to the Office of Management and Budget (OMB)?
    A.   General Accounting Office
    B.   Congressional Budget Office
    C.   Congressional Research Service
    D.   Library of Congress

6.   _____ holds the record for the longest filibuster in the U.S. Senate.
    A.   Alfonse D'Amato
    B.   Robert Byrd
    C.   Ted Stevens
    D.   Strom Thurmond

7.   What proportion of bills require the use of conference committees to iron out differences between the House and Senate?
    A.   About 15 percent
    B.   About 33 percent
    C.   About 60 percent
    D.   About 85 percent

8.   What is the "third house" of the U.S. Congress?
    A.   Staffers
    B.   Interest groups
    C.   Bureaucrats
    D.   Constituents

9.   _____ is the only state with a unicameral legislature.
    A.   Vermont
    B.   North Dakota
    C.   New Mexico
    D.   Nebraska

10.   To serve in the U.S. House, one must be _____ years of age, and _____ years of age to serve in the U.S. Senate.
    A.   20, 25
    B.   25, 30
    C.   30, 35
    D.   35, 40

11.   Which of the following statements is TRUE?
    A.   The House tends to have more rules governing its members than the Senate.
    B.   The House tends to be a more deliberative body than the Senate.
    C.   The House is more insulated from public opinion than the Senate.
    D.   The House leadership has less power over its members than the Senate leadership.

12. Under the original Constitution,
    A. U.S. senators were directly elected by the people.
    B. U.S. senators had four-year terms.
    C. U.S. senators were selected by state legislatures.
    D. U.S. senators were limited to two terms.

13. The power to redraw district lines for the U.S. House rests with
    A. the U.S. Senate.
    B. the Supreme Court.
    C. State legislatures.
    D. the U.S. House.

14. What is the current annual salary for members of the U.S. House and Senate?
    A. $89,900
    B. $136,673
    C. $180,000
    D. $300,000

15. Which of the following statements is TRUE about the U.S. Congress.
    A. When Congress competes with the president, Congress usually wins.
    B. Since the beginning of the republic, Americans have always held Congress in high esteem.
    C. Americans typically approve of the job Congress is doing, but disapprove of the job that their representative is doing.
    D. Americans typically disapprove of the job Congress is doing, but approve of the job that their representative is doing.

16. *Wesberry v. Sanders* (1964) requires
    A. term limits for federal legislators.
    B. state legislatures to create racial and ethnic majority voting districts if feasible.
    C. congressional districts of equal population.
    D. states to implement new voter registration rules.

17. In *Shaw v. Reno* (1993), the Supreme Court
    A. upheld term limits for federal legislators.
    B. allowed a challenge to affirmative action gerrymandering.
    C. allowed a challenge to federal laws governing desegregation in the public schools.
    D. upheld the constitutionality of the death penalty.

18. In 1996, _____ percent of U.S. House and Senate incumbents were reelected.
    A. 40
    B. 66
    C. 82
    D. 95

19. Which of the following statements is TRUE about incumbency?
    A. It is easier to get reelected in the U.S. House than the U.S. Senate.
    B. It is easier to get reelected in the U.S. Senate than the U.S. House.
    C. U.S. House members are more visible than U.S. senators.
    D. Celebrities are more inclined to run for the U.S. House than the U.S. Senate.

20. Former Senate Majority Leader _____ is considered to be an expert parliamentarian and legislative strategist.
    A. Ted Kennedy
    B. Barry Goldwater
    C. Robert Byrd
    D. Al Gore

21. What are the five broad and overlapping functions of the U.S. Congress? Be sure to include a brief discussion of each.

22. What are the four types of committees in the U.S. House and Senate? Be sure to explain the differences between them.

23. What substantial differences remain between the U.S. House and Senate today? Explain.

24. What three patterns of congressional candidate recruitment have emerged in recent years? Explain.

25. With the existence of family stress, fundraising pressures, hyperpartisanship, and institutional gridlock, why do so many members of Congress remain in their positions? Explain.

V.   Critical Thinking Exercises

1. To find out who represents you in the U.S. Congress (if you do not know), simply go to http://www.vote-smart.org. There you can find biographies of national and state leaders, information about campaign finances, issue positions, performance evaluations, and voting records.

2. Select an issue that is compelling to you. Draft a letter to your representative in the U.S. House and both of your U.S. senators. Explain your views on the subject at hand and solicit their perspectives on the same issue. Letters should be addressed in the following manner:

The Honorable _____   The Honorable _____
United States House of Representatives   United States Senate
Washington, D.C. 20515   Washington, D.C. 20510

VI.   Answers to the Practice Exam

1.	A	11.	A
2.	B	12.	C
3.	C	13.	C
4.	C	14.	B
5.	B	15.	D
6.	D	16.	C
7.	A	17.	B
8.	B	18.	D
9.	D	19.	A
10.	B	20.	C

21.   The five broad and overlapping functions of Congress are law making, budget making, representation, executive oversight, and civic education. The most important function of Congress is to make laws. Under Article I of the U.S. Constitution, Congress has both enumerated powers (e.g., power to tax, power to declare war, power to regulate commerce) and implied powers (i.e., to do what is "necessary and proper"). The most important set of bills passed by Congress is the federal budget. This is a policy statement delineating federal public policy priorities through a series of taxing and spending decisions. The third function, representation, is fairly straightforward. Since the United States is a representative democracy, the people elect legislators to make laws on their behalf. In a diverse nation like America, representation is very complex and operates on a variety of levels. A fourth function, executive oversight,

can be highly visible. Congress has a congressional mandate to monitor the activities of the executive branch to see if the laws are being "faithfully executed." Finally, members of Congress are expected to educate people about the legislative process and American politics generally. As such, members meet with constituents, professional lobbyists, and many interest group members who visit them in Washington, D.C. Back home, members report back to their constituents in numerous ways. This allows them to explain the legislative process and their views on public policy to the general public.

22. Both the U.S. House and Senate have four types of committees: standing, joint, conference, and select. Standing committees are the most important, and they are organized around substantive policy subjects. They are permanent committees and there are nineteen in the House and sixteen in the Senate. Standing committees legislate, or process bills. Because they can be rather large, they are divided into subcommittees (committees within committees). There are eighty-six subcommittees in the House and forty-eight in the Senate. Joint committees consist of both senators and representatives, and members are charged with studying various topics that are not necessarily addressed in current legislation. The Joint Economic Committee, for example, studies a range of domestic and international economic issues. A conference committee is a special type of joint committee. It consists of both senators and representatives and their job is very focused–to iron out the differences between similar House and Senate bills and "report out" one compromise bill for both chambers to consider. Select committees are used to investigate particular policy issues or allegations of scandal. The Senate Watergate committee of the 1970s and the Whitewater committee in the 1990s are examples.

23. The substantial differences that exist between the House and Senate revolve around size, representativeness, and tradition. First, size is very important because with 435 members, the House is much more rule-bound than the Senate. Without numerous procedures, floor activity could easily be chaotic. Since the same number of issues are divided among 435 people, House members typically become policy specialists as compared to senators, who are policy generalists. In the 100 member Senate, the legislative process is more deliberative and slow. The leadership has less power over individual senators. Second, representation roles vary between houses. House members represent more narrow, homogeneous populations than the Senate. Senators typically represent larger, more diverse and pluralistic constituencies. Lastly, the tradition of the two chambers is vastly different. Members of the House have always had two year terms and are more attentive to public opinion as a result. Senators are more insulated from public opinion with six year terms and were originally selected by state legislatures until 1913 so that distinguished public figures would be chosen. To this day, Senate membership is considered more prestigious than House membership.

24. Political scientists have identified three emerging patterns of candidate recruitment: self support, party support, and a combination of the two. Some individuals run because they desire to implement their policy preferences or simply to begin political careers. Some already serve in state legislatures or in highly visible local government positions. Some may be familiar with various policy issues, while others self starters may include wealthy individuals who are intent on buying a congressional seat for prestige and other reasons. Another way of emerging as a congressional candidate is to be encouraged by political party officials. In particular, both the Democratic and Republican Senatorial Campaign Committees, the House Democratic Congressional Campaign Committee and the National Republican Congressional Committee scout, encourage, and assist potential candidates. Although political parties would like a greater role in picking and running candidates, congressional elections are now candidate-centered and personal resources, ambition, and attributes are very important. Lastly, in practical terms, most congressional candidates combine self and party support, especially in general elections. Once the primary is over, nominees need money, personal resources, and a great deal of party assistance in order to win.

25.   Despite a lot of pressures, many members remain in their positions for extended periods of time (assuming they are successful at being reelected) for several reasons. One compelling reason is public policy–finding solutions to the nation's policy problems is the primary goal for many members in Congress. Public service motivates such individuals to serve. In order to impact policy, many members astutely aspire to serve on the right committees and to move into leadership positions. To do so, seniority is the primary criterion, so members increase their ability to impact public policy by remaining in their positions for longer periods of time. A second reason is power. Some members seek power within their chamber. The ultimate goal of institutional power is to become a formal leader–such as Speaker of the House or Majority Leader of the Senate. A third reason for maintaining service in either chamber is that there are many benefits that come with the job. Members have an annual salary of $136,673 with generous retirement benefits. They supervise their own bureaucracies on Capitol Hill and back home. They also travel frequently. Capitol Hill has "members only" exercise rooms, swimming pools, and subsidized restaurants. There are also psychic perks–deference is accorded to members by virtually everyone they encounter.

CHAPTER 10
THE PRESIDENCY

I.   Summary

Presidents occupy center stage in American politics, and their powers stem from the U.S. Constitution but their ability to use those powers derives from political and personal resources. Presidential power is paradoxical–Americans expect strong leaders but the political system created by the Framers usually restricts presidents from meeting the expectations of the general public as presidential power is tempered by a system of checks and balances involving Congress and the federal judiciary. Presidents win office by building electoral coalitions; in order to rule effectively, they must form governing coalitions. Once in office, presidents have many different roles including chief of state, commander in chief, chief diplomat, chief executive, and chief legislator. Presidents must contend with the politics of diversity in at least two ways. First, presidential leadership of the nation is more elusive in a more diverse America. There are many specialized audiences in the United States, and they tend to want specialized messages. Such messages tend to alienate groups sooner or later. Second, presidential governance in Washington, D.C. is more elusive in a hyperpluralistic system. Presidents have typically little impact on the relationships between congressional committees and the interest groups that seek to influence them. As a result, hyperpluralism results in political power that is thinly scattered.

II.   Outline

Conclusion: Leadership in a Hyperpluralistic Age (p.282)

III.   Key Terms, Concepts, Events, and People

Be able to identify and/or define each of the following and state its importance in a short paragraph.

Veto power (p.259)

Ordinary vetoes (p.259)

Pocket veto (p.259)

Power of persuasion (p.261)

Political time (p.262)

Presidential clocks (p.262)

Honeymoon period (p.263)

Stewardship theory (p.264)

Plural presidency (p.264)

Postmodern presidency (p.265)

Presidential character (p.265)

Electoral coalition (p.267)

Governing coalition (p.267)

Mandate (p.268)

Foreign policy presidency (p.270)

Domestic policy presidency (p.270)

Economic policy presidency (p.270)

Groupthink (p.270)

Chief of staff (p.272)

Inner cabinet (p.274)

Outer cabinet (p.274)

Executive privilege (p.278)

Diplomacy (p.280)

Military activity (p.280)

Foreign policy doctrines (p.280)

Recognition power (p.280)

Treaties (p.281)

Executive agreements (p.281)

War Powers Act (1973) (p.281)

IV.   Practice Exam

(Answers appear at the end of this chapter)

Multiple Choice

1. The annual salary of U.S. presidents is

    _____.
    A. $100,000
    B. $200,000
    C. $500,000
    D. $1,000,000

2. From George Washington through Bill Clinton's first term, Congress has overturned _____ percent of all regular presidential vetoes.
    A.   7
    B.   25
    C.   50
    D.   65

3. According to political scientist Richard Neustadt, what is the greatest presidential power?
    A.   Commander in chief of the armed forces.
    B.   The power to pardon.
    C.   The power to persuade.
    D.   The power to appoint federal judges.

4. What is a "boll weevil?"
    A.   A liberal Democrat from New England.
    B.   A conservative Democrat from the South.
    C.   A moderate Republican from the industrial Midwest.
    D.   A conservative Republican from the Sunbelt.

5. Which of the following statements is TRUE about the Framers perception of the presidency?
    A.   The Framers believed that the presidency would be the dominant institution of government.
    B.   The Framers believed that presidents would be popular leaders.
    C.   The Framers believed that presidents would be relatively passive clerks.
    D.   The Framers believed that presidents should serve in office for life during good behavior.

6. Which two nineteenth century presidents were exceptions to the first constitutional presidency?
   A. George Washington and Thomas Jefferson
   B. James Monroe and Grover Cleveland
   C. James Madison and Franklin Pierce
   D. Andrew Jackson and Abraham Lincoln

7. _____ first articulated the stewardship theory of the presidency.
   A. George Washington
   B. Abraham Lincoln
   C. Theodore Roosevelt
   D. John Kennedy

8. According to James David Barber, _____ presidents are most successful and best for the nation.
   A. active-negative
   B. passive-positive
   C. passive-negative
   D. active-positive

9. Over the course of American history, nearly _____ percent of presidents were former vice presidents.
   A. 20
   B. 40
   C. 60
   D. 80

10. Which of the following statements is TRUE about vice presidents?
    A. Vice presidents are difficult to beat at the nomination stage.
    B. Vice presidents have a difficult time at the general election stage because they are perceived as followers, not leaders.
    C. Vice presidents do not have much power constitutionally.
    D. All of the above.

11. The chief legislator in the United States is the
    A. president.
    B. Speaker of the House.
    C. Senate Majority Leader.
    D. vice president.

12. Which of the following is NOT an illustration of groupthink?
    A. John Kennedy's Bay of Pigs invasion
    B. Lyndon Johnson's handling of the Vietnam War
    C. George Bush's handling of the Persian Gulf War
    D. Richard Nixon's decisions regarding Watergate

13. Presidential staffing remained minimal until the presidency of _____.
    A. Abraham Lincoln
    B. William McKinley
    C. Franklin Roosevelt
    D. Jimmy Carter

14. _____ concluded that "the president needs help."
    A. The Kerner Commission
    B. The Warren Commission
    C. The Hoover Commission
    D. The Brownlow Commission

15. Which of the following is NOT in the "inner cabinet?"
    A. Secretary of State
    B. Secretary of Interior
    C. Secretary of Treasury
    D. Attorney general

16. Who said that "[m]y country has contrived for me the most insignificant office that ever the invention of man contrived or his imagination conceived?"
    A. Dan Quayle
    B. Walter Mondale
    C. John Nance Garner
    D. John Adams

17. Which of the following statements about public opinion is TRUE?
    A. Over time, public support for the president declines.
    B. Over time, congressional support for the president declines.
    C. Both a + b.
    D. Over time, public support for the president increases.

18. _____ appointed a higher percentage of female federal judges than any other president in history.
    A. John Kennedy
    B. Richard Nixon
    C. Ronald Reagan
    D. Bill Clinton

19. _____ asserted in 1823 that the Western Hemisphere would be closed to further European colonization and aggression.
    A. Thomas Jefferson
    B. James Monroe
    C. Andrew Jackson
    D. William Henry Harrison

20. What policy guided successive presidents until the downfall of the Soviet Union?
    A. The Madison Declaration
    B. The Lincoln Proclamation
    C. The McKinley Doctrine
    D. The Truman Doctrine

Essays

21. What formal powers were given to the president by the Framers in the U.S. Constitution? Be sure to list all of them.

22. According to political scientist James David Barber, presidential character is instrumental in predicting performance in the White House. What is Barber's typology? Be sure to define all four character types and provide examples as well.

23. Discuss the several functional roles of U.S. presidents.

24. Discuss the role of the vice president in the American political system.

25. How have American presidents exercised their national security powers? Explain.

V. Critical Thinking Exercises

1. Similar to the exercise in Chapter 9 where you wrote a letter to your federal representative and senators, write a letter to the president of the United States. Again, select an issue that is compelling to you (perhaps the same issue that you addressed in the previous chapter). Explain your views on the subject at hand and solicit the president's perspectives on the same issue. Letters should be addressed in the following manner:

The Honorable _____
President of the United States
The White House
1600 Pennsylvania Avenue
Washington, D.C. 20500

2.	What qualities (e.g., policy, leadership, character) make for a great president? In your opinion, who was the greatest president in U.S. history? Why? What qualities make for a bad president? In your opinion, who was the worst president in U.S. history? Why? Upon examining the qualities that you deem important, how would you assess the current president?

## VI.	Answers to the Practice Exam

1.	B	11.	A
2.	A	12.	C
3.	C	13.	C
4.	B	14.	D
5.	C	15.	B
6.	D	16.	D
7.	C	17.	C
8.	D	18.	D
9.	A	19.	B
10.	D	20.	D

21.	The Framers of the Constitution did not grant many specific powers to the president compared to Congress. The Framers indicated that the president "shall take Care that the Laws [of Congress] be faithfully executed." They did not define executive power, however. Yet the president's dealings with Congress are not limited to implementing the laws. The president must give a State of the Union message from time to time and presidents also have veto power over legislation that is unacceptable to them. In foreign affairs, the president's powers encompass both military and diplomatic activity. In military matters, the president is the commander in chief of the armed forces, the highest military officer in the government. In diplomatic activities, the president has the power to receive foreign ambassadors. Lastly, the president can grant pardons for federal offenses, except in cases of impeachment. Thus while presidents cannot try cases, they can alter judicial outcomes.

22.	According to James David Barber, presidential character, or the relationship between personality and the job of president, is instrumental in predicting presidential performance. In creating his four character types, he examined two dimensions–activity and affect. Activity refers to the amount of energy that the president invests into the job. Presidents are either active or passive in this regard. Affect refers to whether this activity results in positive or negative satisfaction in one's work. Positive presidents enjoy and even relish their job; negative presidents find it to be a duty, or worse. Based on these four traits, Barber created four character types. Active positive presidents (e.g., Franklin Roosevelt, Harry Truman, John Kennedy, Gerald Ford, Jimmy Carter, and George Bush) enjoy their work, are productive, and readily adapt to change and challenges. Active negative presidents (e.g., Woodrow Wilson, Herbert Hoover, Lyndon Johnson, and Richard Nixon) work hard, get little satisfaction for their hard work, and tend to be compulsive, driven, aggressive, and insecure. Passive positive presidents (e.g., William Howard Taft, Warren Harding, and Ronald Reagan) seek policy agreement, mute dissent, and constantly seek the support of others. They do not work diligently at their jobs, but love the symbolic aspects of politics. Passive negative presidents (e.g., Calvin Coolidge and Dwight Eisenhower) suffer from low self-esteem, abhor politicking, and seem ill-suited for high political office, but serve out of a sense of civic duty. Barber believes that active positive presidents are the most successful; active negative presidents are the worst.

23.	There are several functional roles that U.S. presidents must fulfill simultaneously. First, presidents are chiefs of state meaning that they represent and symbolize the nation to itself and to the world. Second, presidents are commanders in chief. They not only commit troops to combat but are the chief architects of the nation's military policy. Although Congress has the power to declare war under the Constitution, presidents have the ability to make war even without a congressional declaration. Third, presidents are chief diplomats. As such, they maintain channels of negotiation with foreign countries and international organizations. Fourth, presidents are chief executives of a plural presidency consisting of a large federal bureaucracy. Fifth, presidents are chief legislators. Most congressional bills begin as executive branch proposals even though the president cannot constitutionally propose a bill in person in the chamber of the House or Senate. A president can, however, have a "friendly" legislator propose a bill on his/her behalf. Sixth, presidents are the leaders of their own political parties. Presidents are typically chief fund raisers for their parties and they routinely attempt to rejuvenate the party faithful.

24. Constitutionally, the vice president can preside over the Senate and break a tie vote if necessary. Yet vice presidents rarely perform their Senate duties. In reality, the role of the vice president in the American political system depends in large part to the extent that their president is willing to give them substantive responsibilities. Throughout history, vice presidents have complained that their office was insignificant. Yet recent vice presidents have not complained as loudly as their predecessors. While they have tended to attend many state funerals, party gatherings, and various capital functions, they have been given more responsibilities by their bosses than those before them. This is true of Walter Mondale (Carter Administration), Dan Quayle (Bush Administration), and Al Gore (Clinton Administration). Al Gore, for example, is considered to be highly prominent in the Clinton White House in environmental policy, technology concerns, the information superhighway, contracting practices, and government reorganization. Furthermore, Gore has been privy to political and policy strategy sessions, unlike many other vice presidents in U.S. history.

25. U.S. presidents have exercised their national security powers in numerous ways. First, they have developed doctrines or statements to express their foreign policy views (e.g., the Monroe Doctrine in 1823 where President James Monroe asserted that the Western hemisphere would be closed to further European colonization and aggression). Second, presidents have employed their recognition power–the power to receive ambassadors and officially recognize their government. To do so, presidents do not need congressional approval. For example, Jimmy Carter officially recognized the People's Republic of China after decades of nonrecognition. Third, presidents negotiate treaties. This is a shared power with the U.S. Senate because it must ratify treaties. To avoid a treaty defeat in the Senate, some presidents formulate executive agreements. These do not require Senate approval. Fourth, presidents can make war. While Congress has the formal power to declare war under the Constitution, it has not done so many times in American history but presidents have repeatedly used military force nevertheless.

CHAPTER 11
THE BUREAUCRACY

I.   Summary

The federal bureaucracy consists of a wide variety of offices, departments, and agencies. To many it seems very large, but in reality it is far outnumbered by state and local employees. There is no mention of the bureaucracy in the U.S. Constitution, and the growth of this branch could not have been forecasted by the Framers. Similar to the American political system as a whole, the bureaucracy is both diverse and hyperpluralistic in many ways. First, it represents as much as any other branch of government the diversity and particularity of American interest groups. Second, the bureaucracy mirrors the cultural diversity present in the United States. American bureaucrats come from diverse backgrounds and face virtually all the pressures found in society. Third, the entire executive branch of government symbolizes the structural complexity that exists in hyperpluralistic political systems. In a large republic like the United States, the federal bureaucracy must extend its influence in a decentralized manner–typically through field offices scattered all over the nation. Adding to this complexity is the fact that federal rules and regulations are compounded by state and local rules and regulation which helps in understanding why Americans perceive that they are "overregulated."

II.   Outline

III.   Key Terms, Concepts, Events, and People

Be able to identify and/or define each of the following and state its importance in a short paragraph.

Bureaucracy (p.290)

Bureaucrats (p.290)

Bureaucratization (p.290)

Street-level bureaucrats (p.290)

Patronage (p.293)

Pendleton Act (1883) (p.293)

Civil service (p.293)

Civil Service Commission (p.293)

Hatch Act (1939) (p.293)

Civil Service Reform Act (1978) (p.293)

Office of Personnel Management (p.293)

Merit Systems Protection Board (p.293)

Senior Executive Service (p.293)

Economic regulation (p.301)

Social regulation (p.301)

Bureaucratic instinct (p.301)

Territorialism (p.301)

Iron triangles (p.304)

Issue networks (p.304)

Legislative veto (p.306)

Judicial review (p.307)

Administrative law (p.307)

Administrative Procedures Act (1946) (p.307)

Due process (p.307)

Administrative discretion (p.308)

Whistleblowing (p.308)

IV.   Practice Exam

Multiple Choice

1. Not including military personnel, there are about _____ million civilian federal employees.
   A. one
   B. two
   C. three
   D. eight

2. Which of the following is NOT a street-level bureaucrat?
   A. Director of the Environmental Protection Agency
   B. Public school teacher
   C. Police officer
   D. Welfare worker

3. Which of the following was NOT created in 1789?
   A. War Department
   B. State Department
   C. Treasury Department
   D. Justice Department

4. The last agency to become part of the cabinet was
   A. the Department of Education.
   B. the Department of Veterans Affairs.
   C. the Department of Health, Education, and Welfare.
   D. the Department of Defense.

5. In the early years of the republic,
   A. the federal government was staffed by laborers.
   B. the federal government was staffed by highly reputed members of the professional and economic elite.
   C. the federal government did not have any civilian employees.
   D. the federal government had a structured merit system.

6. The impetus for reform of the patronage system
   A. was the assassination of President William McKinley.
   B. was the assassination of President Abraham Lincoln.
   C. was the assassination of President James Garfield.
   D. was the assassination of President John Kennedy.

7. Which of the following was NOT part of the Weberian model of bureaucracy?
   A. Hierarchy
   B. Specialization
   C. Division of labor
   D. Informal rules

8. Federal bureaucracies are creatures of
   A. Congress.
   B. the president.
   C. the Supreme Court.
   D. the general public.

9. Which of the following statements is TRUE about public administrators?
   A. Public administrators do not have a lot of discretion in their jobs.
   B. Public administrators have a lot of discretion in their jobs.
   C. Congress tends to pass broad legislation.
   D. Both b + c.

10. Which of the following departments has the most employees?
    A. Department of Agriculture
    B. Department of Education
    C. Department of Defense
    D. Department of State

11. Which of the following departments spends the most money?
    A. Department of Health and Human Services
    B. Department of Veterans Affairs
    C. Department of Commerce
    D. Department of Interior

12. Which of the following statements is TRUE about the executive bureaucracy?
    A. Women and minorities tend to be overrepresented in the higher ranks of the federal bureaucracy.
    B. Women and minorities tend to be overrepresented in the lower ranks of the federal bureaucracy.
    C. Women and minorities tend to be underrepresented in the higher ranks of the federal bureaucracy.
    D. Both b + c.

13. About _____ percent of all federal employees work and live outside Washington, D.C.
    A. 20
    B. 50
    C. 70
    D. 90

14. Virtually all presidential appointees in the _____ Administration had to pass his antigovernment litmus test.
    A. Kennedy
    B. Carter
    C. Reagan
    D. Clinton

15. The size of the federal bureaucracy shrunk during the _____ years.
    A. Carter
    B. Reagan
    C. Bush
    D. Clinton

16. _____ invalidated the use of the legislative veto in 1983.
    A. Congress
    B. The Supreme Court
    C. The president
    D. The Internal Revenue Service

17. Who has oversight over the federal bureaucracy?
    A. Congress
    B. The president
    C. The federal courts
    D. All of the above.

18. The body of law that encompasses regulatory activity and the judicial review of it is called _____.
    A. constitutional law
    B. administrative law
    C. common law
    D. tort law

19. The actions of administrative agencies are upheld by courts about _____ percent of the time.
    A. 25
    B. 50
    C. 80
    D. 99

20. Which of the following statements is TRUE about whistle-blowing?
    A. Most federal employees hesitate to expose their own agencies' wrongdoing.
    B. Whistle-blowers rarely make enemies within their agencies.
    C. With the passage of the Whistle Blower Protection Act in 1989, whistle-blowing is much more common today than in the past.
    D. Whistle-blowing usually does not occur through leaks to the media, televised interviews, or congressional hearings.

Essays

21. Why is the federal bureaucracy so important in American society, despite the fact that it receives a great deal of criticism? Explain.

22. Identify and explain four theories or models developed by public administration scholars to better understand how bureaucracy works.

23. What are the four broad functions performed by bureaucrats? Be sure to explain each one.

24. How does the federal bureaucracy represent the diversity that exists in the United States? Explain.

25. How would you assess recent presidential attempts to control the federal bureaucracy? Explain.

V.   Critical Thinking Exercises

1. Develop a list of bureaucrats, including street-level bureaucrats, which have made an impact upon your lives in any way. Upon doing so, can you make a generalization about the role of public sector bureaucrats in your individual life? Have the bureaucrats affected you positively or negatively? Explain.

2. Learn more about the president's cabinet by reading information about all fourteen executive departments at http://www.whitehouse.gov/WH/Cabinet/html/cabinet_links.html.

VI.   Answers to the Practice Exam

1.	C	11.	A
2.	A	12.	D
3.	D	13.	D
4.	B	14.	C
5.	B	15.	D
6.	C	16.	B
7.	D	17.	D
8.	A	18.	B
9.	D	19.	C
10.	C	20.	A

21. Most Americans tend to be critical of the federal bureaucracy in general, but have had positive experiences with individual bureaucrats (especially street level bureaucrats). The federal bureaucracy is important in American politics because bureaucrats are responsible for the relatively risk-free lifestyles that Americans enjoy. The same people who have negative perceptions about the bureaucracy expect the federal government to virtually guarantee safe air travel, clean water, clean air, safe workplaces, uncontaminated food, and a host of other safeguards. Government employees are expected to efficiently and expertly educate the nation's children, dispose of waste, protect the environment, defend our freedom, and conquer diseases. When people truly reflect on what government does, they are usually less critical of the bureaucracy. Additionally, bureaucrats are essential for implementing broad and vague legislation. They even implement presidential and judicial policies so absent the bureaucracy, most congressional intentions, presidential decisions, and Supreme Court decrees would never fully take effect.

22. One model developed by public administration scholars is the Weberian model, created by German sociologist Max Weber (1865-1920). He identified several elements of bureaucracy: hierarchy, task specialization, division of labor, and formal rules. Under the Weberian model, employment is based on merit rather than political influence. Weber's model is useful and important to study, but it does not include informal relationships within the organization. As a result, some scholars are compelled by the

acquisitive model. According to this theory, bureaucracies tend to maximize budgets and staff much like private sector companies. Bureaucrats attempt to expand their powers in order to sell their products to consumers. Increasingly, private sector companies compete with government agencies to provide certain services via the privatization process. Those who believe in the garbage can model argue that both the Weberian and the acquisitive models are too neat and tidy, and that large bureaucracies are not as organized, calculating, and purposive as theorists espousing the other models might suggest. According to Charles Lindbloom, bureaucrats "muddle through" and do what they do incrementally. A fourth theory is espoused by James Q. Wilson, who believes that American bureaucracy is uniquely paradoxical (the paradoxical model). Wilson believes that similar to the Weberian model, the bureaucracy is laden with rules, and formality and paperwork are commonplace. On the other hand, American bureaucracy provides ample opportunity for access by individuals and groups–policy activists, advisory boards, citizen groups, congressional investigators, curious journalists, and litigious lawyers. Each of these theories assists us in understanding the complex subject of the federal bureaucracy.

23.   The first broad function of bureaucrats is to implement the law. Federal bureaucrats are creatures of Congress. They must implement or carry out policies established by Congress, the president, and to a lesser extent, the federal judiciary. A second function is to engage in regulation–making, enforcing, and adjudicating various rules. Members of Congress typically pass broadly worded legislation, so it is up to the bureaucrats, through regulations, to carry out the letter and spirit of the law. A third function includes the routine tasks of bureaucracies–administration. Administration includes hiring personnel, giving legal advice, purchasing supplies, and maintaining buildings. A fourth function is representation. While most think of Congress as the "representing branch," executive branch bureaucracies perform this function as well. Bureaucrats represent and even symbolize the goals of Congress, for they implement the laws written by the members who are elected by the people. Bureaucrats also represent their own constituencies or clientele groups. At times, bureaucrats do not simply referee disputes between industries and consumers; in some cases they become advocates of industries and promote an industry's growth and well-being.

24.   The federal bureaucracy represents the diversity in American society in a number of ways. First, most federal employees (about 90 percent) work and live outside the nation's capital in field offices. Researchers have demonstrated that federal workers tend to have more in common with their private sector neighbors than they do with the Washington "establishment." Second, various federal agencies use internal procedures to select their own workers. The sum total of these interagency variations in personnel tends to resemble the diversity that exists in the private sector. Third, like Congress, the executive branch represents and responds to interest group politics. Remember, executive agencies are one of the three components of the iron triangle (interest groups and congressional committees are the other two). The relationship between bureaucrats and their client constituencies is symbiotic. If budget cuts are rumored, interest groups typically rush to the agency's defense. In turn, federal administrators often act as advocates for the interest groups that support them.

25.   Presidents of both major political parties have expressed a great deal of frustration regarding their inability to control their own federal bureaucracy. In his last year as president, Jimmy Carter summed up this frustration: "Before I became president, I realized and was warned that dealing with the federal bureaucracy would be one of the worst problems I would have to face. It has been worse than I had anticipated." Presidents generally become frustrated because they perceive that all federal bureaucrats should be accountable to them, yet many bureaucrats perceive the president as a short-term occupant of the White House who is preoccupied with issues more important than bureaucratic accountability. Recent approaches to controlling the federal bureaucracy have varied a bit. President Nixon attempted to end leaks and other forms of bureaucratic mischief. He also tried to create a supercabinet by combining existing departments, but Congress rejected the idea. Ronald Reagan attempted to control the bureaucrats by utilizing an antigovernment litmus test for virtually all presidential appointees. In so doing, he insured

that the upper echelon in most executive agencies adhered to administration policy. When top civil service positions became available, he placed political appointees into these spots as well. Bill Clinton had a different priority when he became president. He wanted to appoint more women and minorities to executive branch positions. By 1994, he appointed a higher percentage of women than any other president in history. He also wanted to "reinvent government" by cutting inefficiency and waste. In so doing, the federal bureaucracy shrunk during the Clinton years as compared to the Reagan/Bush era when the federal bureaucracy actually increased in size.

CHAPTER 12
THE JUDICIARY

I.   Summary

American government is premised on the rule of law and comes from a variety of sources including Supreme Court decisions, lower court rulings, legislative statutes, and administrative regulations. Litigation involves both civil and criminal cases. The American legal system is actually 51 systems (1 federal and 50 state) featuring an adversarial process, judicial review, the rule of precedent, the doctrine of original intent, a distinct legal culture, and the notion of jury justice. The American judiciary both contributes to and is affected by diversity and political hyperpluralism. There is an ample body of laws to apply and plenty of disputes to resolve. Simply the way American courts are organized contributes to judicial fragmentation and hyperpluralism as many cases can either be filed in federal or state court, and many are interest group driven and sponsored. American courts contribute to diversity because local and regional factors, party affiliation, gender, race, ethnicity, and judicial federalism affect judicial decision making.

II.   Outline

The Courts in Action: *Romer v. Evans* (p.314)
Introduction: The Law and American Politics (p.315)
      Rule of Law (p.316)
      Sources of Law (p.316)
      How Litigious Are We? (p.317)
Features of the American Legal System (p.317)
      Adversarial Justice (p.318)
      Judicial Review (p.318)
      Rule of Precedent (p.319)
      Original Intent (p.319)
      The Legal Culture (p.320)
      Jury Justice (p.321)
How Courts Are Organized (p.322)
      State Courts (p.322)
      Federal Courts (p.323)
      U.S. Supreme Court (p.325)
      The Journey of a Supreme Court Case (p.325)
Becoming a Judge or Justice (p.327)
      State Courts (p.328)
      Federal Courts (p.328)
      U.S. Supreme Court (p.329)
How Courts Make Policy (p.331)
      Trial Courts (p.331)
      Appellate Courts (p.331)
      U.S. Supreme Court (p.332)
      Limits on Judicial Activism (p.334)
Sources of Judicial Diversity (p.335)

III.   Key Terms, Concepts, Events, and People

Be able to identify and/or define each of the following and state its importance in a short paragraph.

American legalism (p.316)

Constitutional law (p.316)

Statutory law (p.316)

Judicial law (p.316)

Common law (p.316)

Administrative law (p.316)

Judicial review (p.318)

Writ of mandamus (p.318)

Rule of precedent (p.319)

Doctrine of original intent (p.319)

Strict constructionists (p.320)

Legal culture (p.320)

Assumption of guilt (p.321)

Grand juries (p.321)

Petit juries (p.321)

Bench trials (p.321)

Jury nullification (p.321)

Overlapping jurisdiction (p.322)

Concurrent jurisdiction (p.322)

Diversity cases (p.322)

District courts (p.323)

Intermediate appellate courts (p.323)

Writ of certiorari (p.325)

Amicus curiae briefs (p.326)

Concurring opinion (p.326)

Dissenting opinion (p.327)

Senatorial courtesy (p.328)

Judicial activism (p.330)

Judicial restraint (p.331)

Incorporation doctrine (p.332)

Judicial implementation (p.334)

Judicial diversity (p.335)

Judicial localism (p.335)

Judicial federalism (p.337)

IV.   Practice Exam

(Answers appear at the end of this chapter)

Multiple Choice

1. The primary source of American law is
   A. the U.S. Constitution.
   B. English common law.
   C. federal statutory law.
   D. state statutory law.

2. Which of the following statements is TRUE?
   A. Most cases in the U.S. are resolved by federal courts.
   B. Most cases in the U.S. are resolved by state courts.
   C. American litigation rates are much higher than other democracies.
   D. Both a + c.

3. According to Alexander Hamilton, the _____ branch of government was inherently the weakest.
   A. legislative
   B. executive
   C. judicial
   D. administrative

4. _____ declared that "[i]t is emphatically the province and duty of the judicial department to say what the law is."
   A. Alexander Hamilton
   B. Thomas Jefferson
   C. James Madison
   D. John Marshall

5. How did the U.S. Supreme Court obtain the power of judicial review?
   A. It was granted in Article III of the U.S. Constitution.
   B. It was granted by an act of Congress.
   C. It was granted by an executive order.
   D. The Supreme Court granted itself the power.

6. The vast majority of all jury criminal trials worldwide occur in _____.
   A. Belgium
   B. the People's Republic of China
   C. the United States
   D. Australia

7. The most frequent litigant in federal cases
   A. is the federal government itself.
   B. is the state of Maine.
   C. is the tobacco lobby.
   D. is the National Rifle Association.

8. How do cases get put on the Supreme Court's docket?
   A. The rule of four.
   B. It is up to the Chief Justice.
   C. The rule of five.
   D. It is up to the justice who has served the longest tenure.

9. Each case is allotted _____ for oral argument in the U.S. Supreme Court.
   A. one month
   B. one week
   C. one day
   D. one hour

10. The U.S. Supreme Court begins its new term in _____.
    A. December
    B. October
    C. July
    D. January

11. Which of the following statements is TRUE about federal judges?
    A. They serve 10 year terms.
    B. They serve 6 year terms.
    C. They serve 2 year terms.
    D. They serve for life.

110

12. In 1987, the U.S. Senate rejected the appointment of _____ to the U.S. Supreme Court.
    A. Lewis Powell
    B. Robert Bork
    C. Thurgood Marshall
    D. David Souter

13. The _____ Court is remembered for strongly supporting national power over states' rights.
    A. Ellsworth
    B. Marshall
    C. Taney
    D. Warren

14. The _____ Court is remembered for expanding civil rights and liberties.
    A. Rehnquist
    B. Burger
    C. Warren
    D. Hughes

15. The ability of the federal judiciary to make policy
    A. is unlimited.
    B. is limited by state legislators.
    C. is limited by public opinion.
    D. is limited by the liberal media.

16. The most liberal group of federal judges are
    A. Northern Democrats.
    B. Southern Democrats.
    C. Northern Republicans.
    D. Southern Republicans.

17. Prior to the Fourteenth Amendment, the Supreme Court's workload was dominated by
    A. public law matters.
    B. private law matters.
    C. civil liberties issues.
    D. civil rights issues.

18. What happened after the Supreme Court decided *Brown v. Board of Education* (1954)?
    A. Southern school systems desegregated very quickly.
    B. Northern school systems desegregated very quickly.
    C. States and school districts took decades to even begin implementing desegregation.
    D. All school systems desegregated by 1960.

19. What is the most undemocratic institution at the federal level?
    A. U.S. Senate
    B. U.S. House of Representatives
    C. U.S. president
    D. U.S. Supreme Court

20. The U.S. Supreme Court was created by
    A. Article III of the U.S. Constitution.
    B. Article II of the U.S. Constitution.
    C. Article I of the U.S. Constitution.
    D. the Judiciary Act of 1789.

Essays

21. Are Americans much more litigious than citizens in other Western democracies? Why or why not?

22. How did the Supreme Court obtain the power of judicial review? Explain.

23. What do critics posit about the doctrine of original intent? Why?

24. When the justices of the Supreme Court decide to set a case for hearing, what happens? Explain all the steps and procedures involved.

25. What are the limits on judicial activism? Explain.

V. Critical Thinking Exercises

1. Select any Supreme Court decision and read it. Identify the facts of the case, the Court's decision, and the opinion of the Court. Scrutinize the judicial reasoning employed. What is your opinion of the Court's interpretation of the Constitution and/or statutory law? Explain.

2. Many scholars debate the plausibility of judicial activism versus judicial restraint. What is your opinion on these differing judicial philosophies? What is the proper role of federal judges in American politics? Be sure to carefully explain your reasoning.

VI. Answers to the Practice Exam

1.	A	11.	D
2.	B	12.	B
3.	C	13.	B
4.	D	14.	C
5.	D	15.	C
6.	C	16.	A
7.	A	17.	B
8.	A	18.	C
9.	D	19.	D
10.	B	20.	A

21. By most criteria, the United States is certainly a litigious society. Caseloads have increased sharply in both federal and state courts over the last several decades. Yet compared to other Western democracies, the United States is less litigious than many analysts assume. To be sure, people rely on courts to solve a wide variety of simple and complex personal and business problems in a large advanced industrial democracy. But the United States may be less litigious than is commonly perceived. First of all, although many cases are filed, far fewer actually go to trial. Second, many people for various reasons actually avoid litigation even though many perceive the opposite to be true. Third, although the absolute number of lawsuits has increased dramatically, the rate of litigation has not (the number of cases per 1000 people). Fourth, compared to other Western democracies, rates of litigation in the United States are not dissimilar. The rate in the United States is about the same that exists in Canada, Australia, England, and New Zealand.

22. The Supreme Court obtained the power of judicial review formally in 1803, when the decision in *Marbury v. Madison* was announced. In the national elections in 1800, the Federalists lost control of the presidency and both houses of Congress to Jeffersonian Republicans. Before leaving office, President John Adams and the lame-duck Federalist Congress rushed to appoint Federalists to newly-created federal judgeships. In the case of the midnight judges, time literally ran out on the Adams Administration. Some of the judicial commissions remained on the desk of the Federalist Secretary of State John Marshall, who did not sign or deliver them. Incoming President Thomas Jefferson instructed his new Secretary of State, James Madison, to not deliver them. Marbury and his peers sued for their positions. Specifically, they sought a writ of mandamus from the Supreme Court to order Madison to perform the task of signing and delivering the judicial commissions. Under the Judiciary Act of 1789, the Supreme Court had original jurisdiction in the case. No lower court reviewed the case. Yet the new Chief Justice, John Marshall, convinced the other justices that this section of the Judiciary Act was unconstitutional because it gave the Court a power that contradicted Article III of the Constitution. The Court therefore struck down this part of the Judiciary Act and in so doing, granted itself the power of judicial review–the power to say what a law means and what it means not.

23. Those who believe in the doctrine of original intent attempt to apply the Constitution to various cases and situations by asking, "What did the Framers mean? What did they intend?" Seeking the intent of the Framers requires judges to examine not only constitutional wording but also to take account of the debates at the Philadelphia Convention as well as the *Federalist Papers*. Those who subscribe to this doctrine maintain that the Framers selected their words carefully and we should consider their intent in a much different world. The doctrine of original intent has many critics. First, they ask "Who were the Framers?" Not all of the delegates in Philadelphia stayed the entire time; others did not participate actively in the debates. Second, the Framers disagreed on many issues. As a result, some decisions resulted in compromises that many did not like. Determining original intent in that context seems to be a fairly meaningless activity. Third, critics contend that strict constructionists use original intent to justify their own ideological views and policy preferences. Lastly, critics of the doctrine of original intent maintain that the Constitution is a "living document," and should change with the times in order to benefit future Americans.

24. When the justices of the Supreme Court decide to set a case for hearing, many things happen. First, the parties to the case file new briefs that focus only on questions of law. Interest groups also refile *amicus* briefs at this stage. Controversial cases such as *Webster v. Reproductive Health Services* (1989) attract large numbers of them. Second, oral argument takes place. Oral argument is very limited by the justices–one hour is allocated per case, meaning that each side has only 30 minutes. The justices freely interrupt the lawyers with questions and/or comments. The justices therefore control the direction of the oral argument. Third, the Court discusses in conference the cases that are heard that week. The chief justice summarizes the case and in order of seniority, the justices share their perspectives on the cases. Upon doing so, the justices vote. If the chief justice votes with the majority, he/she assigns the task of writing the majority opinion. If he/she is in the minority, the most senior justice on the majority side assigns that task.

25. Judicial activism can occur on the part of either liberal or conservative judges. While many perceive that the power of judicial review is unfettered, the power of federal judges to make policy is limited by three different forces. First, federal judges can meet with congressional resistance. This occurs when Supreme Court nominees are scrutinized by the U.S. Senate (e.g., Robert Bork and Clarence Thomas). The Senate can also resist acting upon presidential appointments to the district courts and courts of appeal. Congress also has the constitutional power to restructure the courts. Second, another limit on judicial power is the reality that most decisions are easier to make than implement. Three groups (an interpreting population including judges and lawyers, an implementing population including state and local officials, and a consuming population including the general public) can resist implementing judicial decrees. Third, public opinion may be the most significant constraint on judicial power. Some research suggests that many court decisions conform to the demands and desires of the people. By way of example, the Supreme Court is more likely to overturn state and local laws that deviate from national public opinion.

CHAPTER 13
CIVIL LIBERTIES AND RIGHTS

I.   Summary

An overview of the public policy making process is provided in this chapter, including a discussion of the steps involved: problem identification, policy formulation, policy adoption, policy implementation, and policy evaluation. There are three broad types of policies (civil liberties and civil rights, domestic policy, and foreign policy). Civil liberties are areas of personal freedoms enjoyed by individual Americans. Civil rights relates to equal treatment sought by different groups of Americans. The cornerstone of civil liberties and rights in the United States is the Constitution. The Supreme Court at one time only applied the Bill of Rights to Congress; in this century it has become gradually applied to the states as well. There is a natural chronology to liberties and rights–liberties come first, followed typically by a civil rights struggle in order to fully implement liberties for all groups in American society. In the hyperpluralistic system in the United States, the quest for liberties and rights is a source of unending conflict.

II.   Outline

III.   Key Terms, Concepts, Events, and People

Be able to identify and/or define each of the following and state its importance in a short paragraph.

Communications Decency Act (p.345)

Policy agenda (p.347)

Policy cornerstones (p.347)

Dominant policy actors (p.348)

Policy actions (p.348)

Civil liberties (p.349)

Civil rights (p.349)

Ex post facto laws (p.349)

Bills of attainder (p.349)

Writs of habeas corpus (p.349)

Dual citizenship (p.350)

Religious Freedom Restoration Act (1993) (p.355)

Political speech (p.356)

Public speech (p.356)

Symbolic speech (p.356)

Prior restraint (p.357)

Exclusionary rule (p.359)

Eminent domain (p.361)

Legal equality (p.364)

Equality of opportunity (p.364)

Equality of condition (p.364)

Affirmative action (p.366)

Equal Rights Amendment (p.367)

Americans with Disabilities Act of 1990 (p.370)

Age Discrimination in Employment Act (1967) (p.370)

IV.   Practice Exam

(Answers appear at the end of this chapter)

Multiple Choice

1. Civil rights policy
    A. protects individual freedoms.
    B. grants fair and equal treatment to Americans.
    C. is best illustrated by the First Amendment.
    D. Both a + c.

2. The cornerstone of domestic policy is
    A. the Constitution.
    B. the economy.
    C. the Bill of Rights.
    D. statutory law.

3. The first step in the public policy process is
    A. policy formulation.
    B. policy adoption.
    C. policy implementation.
    D. problem identification.

4. The _____ Amendment contained the language to nationalize the Bill of Rights.
    A. First
    B. Fifth
    C. Tenth
    D. Fourteenth

5. The _____ Amendment is the most visible illustration of a civil liberty in the United States.
    A. First
    B. Second
    C. Ninth
    D. Sixteenth

6. _____ prohibited racial discrimination throughout American society based on race, religion, sex, or national origin.
    A. The Voting Rights Act of 1965
    B. The Civil Rights Act of 1957
    C. The Civil Rights Act of 1964
    D. The Americans with Disabilities Act of 1990

7. Which of the following statements is NOT true?
    A. Public aid for religiously-oriented schools is allowed if it serves a secular or neutral purpose.
    B. Activity at public schools must be religiously neutral.
    C. Prayer and Bible reading in public schools is allowed.
    D. Traditionally, the South has been the Bible Belt in the United States.

8. _____ created the "clear and present danger" free speech standard.
    A. Oliver Wendell Holmes
    B. William Howard Taft
    C. Willis Van Devanter
    D. Felix Frankfurter

9. What did the Supreme Court rule in *Texas v. Johnson* (1989)?
    A. Burning the American flag is protected under free speech.
    B. Voluntary school prayers are protected under the First Amendment.
    C. Prior restraint violates the First Amendment.
    D. News organizations have an absolute right to cover courtroom trials.

10. The Supreme Court established the right to free legal counsel in all state criminal cases in _____.
    A. *Betts v. Brady*
    B. *Escobedo v. Illiniois*
    C. *Gideon v. Wainwright*
    D. *Miranda v. Arizona*

11. The Supreme Court temporarily struck down the death penalty in _____.
    A. *Furman v. Georgia*
    B. *Mapp v. Ohio*
    C. *New York Times v. Sullivan*
    D. *New York Times v. United States*

12. The Supreme Court reinstated the death penalty in _____.
    A. *Furman v. Georgia*
    B. *Gregg v. Georgia*
    C. *Hawaii Housing Authority v. Midkiff*
    D. *Griswold v. Connecticut*

13. A specific right to privacy in the Constitution was established in

    _____.
    A. *Bowers v. Hardwick*
    B. *Cruzan v. Director, Missouri Department of Health*
    C. *Griswold v. Connecticut*
    D. *Washington v. Glucksberg*

14. Contemporary abortion policy in the United States was created by
    A. the president.
    B. Congress.
    C. the Supreme Court.
    D. the state legislatures.

15. In 1857, _____ declared that slaves were "beings of an inferior order."
    A. the Supreme Court
    B. Congress
    C. the president
    D. Dred Scott

16. The Supreme Court upheld segregation as constitutional in _____.
    A. *Dred Scott v. Sanford*
    B. *Plessy v. Ferguson*
    C. *Brown v. Board of Education*
    D. *Swann v. Charlotte-Mecklenberg Board of Education*

17. The use of explicit racial quotas was banned by the Supreme Court in _____.
    A. *Regents of the University of California v. Bakke*
    B. *Plessy v. Ferguson*
    C. *Munn v. Illinois*
    D. *Frontiero v. Richardson*

18. The Equal Rights Amendment was ratified by _____ states after it passed Congress in 1972.
    A. 0
    B. 15
    C. 35
    D. 48

19. The Equal Pay Act, passed in _____, required women and men to be paid equally if their jobs were equal.
    A. 1873
    B. 1906
    C. 1945
    D. 1963

20. In _____, the Supreme Court upheld the practice of relocating West Coast Americans of Japanese descent as constitutional.
    A. *Plyler v. Doe*
    B. *Lau v. Nichols*
    C. *Rotsker v. Goldberg*
    D. *Korematsu v. United States*

Essays

21. Detail each stage of the public policy making process.

22. Explain why the civil liberties and rights policy process is triangular, similar to the iron triangle consisting of congressional committees, executive agencies, and interest groups.

23. To many, freedom of the press is an absolute right. Is this the case? Why or why not?

24. What safeguards are involved in a fair trial? Explain.

25. Explain how, and under what circumstances, the Supreme Court was responsible for upholding and then nullifying segregation in the United States.

V. Critical Thinking Exercises

1. Research the background and origin of the Second Amendment. Try to discern the intent of the amendment when it was added to the Constitution in 1791, and how it should be applied to society today. Upon doing so, are you inclined to support or oppose gun control legislation? Why or why not?

2. Does equality of opportunity exist in the United States for all groups? Be sure to defend your thesis with concrete evidence, one way or another.

VI. Answers to the Practice Exam

1.	B	11.	A
2.	B	12.	B
3.	D	13.	C
4.	D	14.	C
5.	A	15.	A
6.	C	16.	B
7.	C	17.	A
8.	A	18.	C
9.	A	19.	D
10.	C	20.	D

21. The first stage of the public policy making process is problem identification. The problem is identified at this stage, defined, and redefined. The second stage is policy formulation. Once a problem has been recognized, alternative policy proposals are drafted and their relative advantages and disadvantages discussed. The third stage is policy adoption. Ultimately, the adoption of a public policy involves making some decision or taking some action. Many such decisions may be very minor and incremental in nature. Policy implementation is the fourth stage. This entails actually executing the policy, or carrying it out. It includes such things as enforcing decisions, spending money, writing regulations, administering programs, or even deploying troops, depending on the situation. The final stage is policy evaluation, which is retrospective. Policy makers at this stage attempt to ascertain the relative effectiveness of the policy by some established criteria.

22. The civil liberties and rights policy process is triangular, as the triangle itself represents many diverse interests in the American hyperpluralistic system. The first point of the triangle consists of individual litigants and/or interest groups which operate on their behalf. These people have real cases or problems that need to be resolved. Yet few civil liberties and rights claimants can afford to take their own case or cause through the judicial system. This is why many groups do so on their behalf. The second point consists of the state and federal judiciary. The courts, and ultimately the U.S. Supreme Court, are increasingly resolving controversies regarding civil liberties and civil rights. At one time, civil liberties and rights cases only represented about 2-3 percent of the Supreme Court's overall caseload. Now, the figure is typically between 10-25 percent. The third point in the triangle consists of a variety of governmental agencies which support, augment, or implement the work of the judiciary. By way of example, Congress plays a major role on occasion by passing major civil rights legislation, such as the Civil Rights Act of 1964.

23. Freedom of the press may seem absolute but no rights are absolute. Limits involving sex, libel, and the courts serve to constrain the press. First, the press is not constitutionally protected when it publishes sexually obscene materials. Yet ascertaining the meaning of obscene has proven to be a most daunting task for judges. Second, libel–the publication of false or maliciously written statements–is not protected by the Constitution. To prove libel, however, plaintiffs must "show actual malice" and do so with "convincing clarity." Third, freedom of the press does not extend to courts of law. At times, the Sixth Amendment right to a fair trial is weighed against freedom of the press. The Supreme Court has determined that reporters can be forced to divulge what they know about a crime based on their interviews with suspects. Furthermore, news organizations do not have an absolute right to cover courtroom trials.

24. Fair trials must have many safeguards. First, they cannot be delayed too long or drag on too long. According to the Sixth Amendment, the accused have the right to a "speedy" trial. As a result, criminal trials must be heard before civil trials, so civil trials can be delayed for a number of years in some places. Second, juries cannot be selected using discriminatory practices. Third, juries need to be large enough to allow for deliberation and to adequately represent the community. Fourth, juries decisions usually need to be unanimous. Fifth, defendants must be able to confront witnesses and not be forced to testify against themselves. As a result, very few criminal defendants take the stand and they cannot be forced to do so.

25. In 1896, the Supreme Court ruled that segregation did not violate the U.S. Constitution in *Plessy v. Ferguson*. According to the majority opinion, "If one race be inferior than the other socially, the Constitution of the United States cannot put them upon the same plane..." The lone dissenter, Justice John Marshall Harlan, argued that "In the view of the Constitution, in the eye of the law, there is in this country no superior, dominant, ruling class of citizens. There is no caste here. Our Constitution is colorblind, and neither knows nor tolerates classes among citizens." Harlan's dissent in 1896 became the law of the land 58 years later when the Court rendered its decision in *Brown v. Board of Education*. A unanimous Court through Chief Justice Earl Warren ruled that the "separate but equal" standard created in *Plessy* was unconstitutional under the equal protection clause of the Fourteenth Amendment. According to Warren, "We conclude that in the field of public education, the doctrine of 'separate but equal' has no place. Separate but equal educational facilities are inherently unequal." Thus, the Supreme Court formally ended the practice of segregation in the United States.

CHAPTER 14
DOMESTIC POLICY: THE COST OF DIVERSITY

I.   Summary

Domestic policy in the United States encompasses numerous laws, programs, and governmental actions that profoundly affect the lives of American citizens. Virtually all domestic policy issues involve money, and in the American hyperpluralistic system, some groups benefit from governmental decision making, and others pay for it. In the United States, domestic policy is structurally fragmented both horizontally (across three branches of government) and vertically (between the federal and state and local governments). The premier public policy statement is the federal budget, which outlines the policy priorities of the federal government which has a significant impact on the domestic economy and society as a whole.

II.   Outline

III.   Key Terms, Concepts, Events, and People

Be able to identify and/or define each of the following and state its importance in a short paragraph.

Mixed economy (p.381)

Gross national product (GNP) (p.381)

Gross domestic product (GDP) (p.381)

Index of Leading Economic Indicators (p.381)

Unemployment (p.381)

Inflation (p.382)

Consumer Price Index (CPI) (p.382)

COLAs (p.382)

Budget process (p.383)

Fiscal year (FY) (p.383)

Budget cycle (p.383)

Budget resolution (p.384)

Authorization bills (p.384)

Appropriation bills (p.384)

Discretionary spending (p.384)

Direct spending (p.384)

Trust funds (p.384)

Continuing resolutions (p.384)

Federal budget deficit (p.385)

Federal debt (p.385)

Excise taxes (p.385)

Tax expenditures (p.385)

Flat tax (p.387)

Cruise control spending (p.387)

Entitlements (p.387)

Ambivalent benevolence (p.388)

Deserving needy (p.388)

Undeserving needy (p.388)

Preventative strategies (p.388)

Curative strategies (p.388)

Social insurance (p.389)

Managed care (p.391)

Absolute poverty (p.393)

Relative poverty (p.393)

Feminization of poverty (p.394)

Personal Responsibility and Work Opportunity Act of 1996 (p.394)

Workfare (p.395)

Working poor (p.396)

Homeless (p.397)

Accumulated fragmentation (p.400)

Command and control approach (p.401)

Direct regulation (p.402)

Marriage Protection Act (1996) (p.403)

Third-rail issues (p.404)

IV.   Practice Exam

(Answers appear at the end of this chapter)

Multiple Choice

1. What is the premier policy statement of the federal government?
   A. The budget
   B. The Social Security program
   C. The Medicare program
   D. Foreign policy expenditures

2. What is the fiscal year for the federal government?
   A. January 1-December 31
   B. April 1-March 31
   C. July 1-June 30
   D. October 1-September 30

3. About _____ percent of all federal revenue comes from the individual income tax.
   A. 12
   B. 39
   C. 55
   D. 67

4. About _____ percent of all federal revenue comes from corporate income taxes.
   A. 2
   B. 11
   C. 25
   D. 42

5. The federal debt is currently more than _____ dollars.
   A. 225 billion
   B. 500 billion
   C. 1.5 trillion
   D. 5 trillion

6. _____ is the largest entitlement program in the United States.
   A. Medicare
   B. Medicaid
   C. Social Security
   D. AFDC

7. Currently, about _____ percent of the federal budget goes to pay interest on the national debt.
   A. 1
   B. 6
   C. 15
   D. 33

8. The federal government currently spends about _____ per year.
   A. $500 billion
   B. $1.1 trillion
   C. $1.7 trillion
   D. $3.3 trillion

9. _____ argued that Social Security would protect Americans from the "hazards and vicissitudes of life."
   A. Calvin Coolidge
   B. Herbert Hoover
   C. Harry Truman
   D. Franklin Roosevelt

10. _____ spends more per capita on health care than any other nation in the world.
    A. Sweden
    B. Canada
    C. Germany
    D. The United States

11. In 1998, the poverty standard for a family of four in the continental United States was _____.
    A. $8,650
    B. $16,450
    C. $26,500
    D. $40,000

12. Among the states, the poverty rate is the highest in _____.
    A. Maine
    B. Indiana
    C. Mississippi
    D. New Mexico

13. At its highest level, federal aid has accounted for _____ percent of the total costs of elementary and secondary education.
    A. 10
    B. 25
    C. 50
    D. 75

128

14. _____ laid the theoretical foundation for the New Deal.
   A. Marxism
   B. Socialism
   C. Keynesianism
   D. Monetarism

15. _____ has the power to establish monetary policy in the United States.
   A. The president
   B. Congress
   C. The Internal Revenue Service
   D. The Federal Reserve Board

16. _____ is the primary federal agency responsible for environmental regulation.
   A. The Sierra Club
   B. The Environmental Protection Agency
   C. The Interior Department
   D. The Wildlife Department

17. Which of the following is an illustration of symbolic regulation?
   A. Tobacco regulation
   B. "Just Say No" to drugs
   C. "The era of big government is over"
   D. Both b + c

18. _____ regulates the tobacco companies.
   A. The Food and Drug Administration
   B. Congress
   C. The Office of Management and Budget
   D. The Department of Health and Human Services

19. Direct regulation does NOT involve
   A. rewards.
   B. punishments.
   C. restraints.
   D. just "speaking out" against something.

20. Which of the following is TRUE about American public opinion.
   A. Americans believe that there is too much regulation in the United States.
   B. Americans support entitlement programs, but not higher taxes to pay for them.
   C. Americans believe that the federal government is too big.
   D. All of the above.

Essays

21. According to political scientist James Q. Wilson, what are the four political patterns which help to explain how many groups coalesce around various policy issues? Be sure to explain each one.

22. Why do Americans tend to disagree over regulatory policy? Explain.

23. Why can the politics of environmental protection best be described as accumulated fragmentation? Explain.

24. What are four separate but interrelated approaches to environmental protection used by federal and state officials? Explain.

25. What methods are used in employing direct regulation? Explain.

V.   Critical Thinking Exercises

1. As discussed in the text, the poverty standard in the United States for a family of four in 1998 was $16,450 (it is slightly higher in Alaska and Hawaii). Critique the federal government's definition of

poverty. Is it too high, just about right, or too low? Why?

2.   Political conservatives tend to advocate state and local control of elementary and secondary education with little or no involvement by the federal government. Liberals tend to support a more active federal involvement in public education. Which side, if any, is right in this policy dispute? Explain why using concrete illustrations.

VI.   Answers to the Practice Exam

1.	A	11.	B
2.	D	12.	C
3.	B	13.	A
4.	B	14.	C
5.	D	15.	D
6.	C	16.	B
7.	C	17.	D
8.	C	18.	A
9.	D	19.	D
10.	D	20.	D

21.   According to James Q. Wilson, the four political patterns which help explain how many groups coalesce around various policy issues are client, entrepreneurial, interest group, and majoritarian. Client politics occurs when a small group stands to benefit from a particular policy and the costs of such policies are paid for by society as a whole. In entrepreneurial politics, coalitions form around a relatively small handful of individuals who claim to speak for a much larger number of people. They advocate policies which benefit the "silent majority" while imposing costs elsewhere. Interest group politics entails a competition between and among diverse interests to influence the policy making process. It occurs when one group stands to gain from a particular policy and another stands to lose. Majoritarian politics occurs when a large majority of people believe they will benefit from a particular policy and are willing to pay the costs associated with it. To varying degrees, all four patterns occur in American politics.

22.   In the American hyperpluralistic system, citizens tend to disagree over regulatory policy. An important reason which helps in understanding this phenomenon is that different people tend to ask different types of questions concerning regulation. Among the differing questions include the following: (1) Is government regulation needed or should the private sector take care of itself; (2) Which public goals are most important; (3) Which level of regulation–federal, state, or local–is most appropriate; (4) Should government regulation proceed slowly, incrementally, or rapidly; and (5) Are there effective alternatives to government regulation?

23.   There are two major reasons why the politics of environmental protection can best be described as accumulated fragmentation. First, new environmental issues are routinely added to the ones that already exist, so the amount of regulation in an advanced industrialized nation like the United States keeps increasing. In order to protect the water and air supply in the United States, the government must constantly monitor the activities of industries. At the same time, new threats to the environment surface continuously. Second, the environmental policy making process in a federal form of government is very fragmented. There are really two forms of fragmentation in the United States–horizontal and vertical. Horizontal fragmentation refers to divided policy responsibility across various agencies, especially at the federal level. While the Environmental Protection Agency (EPA) is the chief agency empowered with regulating the environment, it is not the only one. Vertical fragmentation is evident in the fact that the states all have differing versions of the federal EPA, and often have their own approaches to environmental protection. Some states exceed federal requirements, while others view federal policy

making as an usurpation of state sovereignty. Added to all this jurisdictional fragmentation are thousands of interest groups at all three levels of government.

24. All four approaches to environmental protection used by federal and state officials are all based on one fundamental truth: the private sector largely creates pollution, but it is the government's responsibility to eliminate it. The approaches tend to reflect client politics or interest group politics. The traditional approach is to regulate the private sector–standards are established by the government and offenders are ordered to comply. This is commonly called the command and control approach, where noncompliance results in fines or other sanctions. A second approach is to play the "move it" game, which is commonly used by states and local governments. For example, states with stringent environmental laws may, in effect, encourage businesses to export their pollution to other states. Furthermore, local activists have succeeded in moving projects like hazardous waste treatment plants outside their own jurisdictions. Sometimes, these projects move to minority communities–a process minorities call "environmental racism." A third approach is to price it–to affix a value to such entities as water, clean air, or even pollution. By setting a price on such commodities, the government can induce the private sector to offset existing sources of pollution. This pricing approach is one of the components of the 1990 version of the Clean Air Act, where companies that met federal emission standards were allowed to sell or trade "pollution credits" to other companies facing regulation. A final approach is to replace environmentally hazardous fossil fuels and traditional hydroelectric power with renewable energy sources such as the wind and the sun. Progress has been slow in developing this technology, however.

25. Direct regulation employs one of four methods–information, rewards, restraints, or punishments. One method of regulation is to require manufacturers to provide consumers with certain information (e.g., nutritional information on food labels, cancer warnings on tobacco products). Such labeling allows consumers to make more informed judgements about using the products in question. A second method of regulation is to use rewards to encourage people to do what they might not otherwise do. The government, for example, grants subsidies to certain groups such as farmers to encourage them to grow certain crops. A third method is to use restraints to curtail certain practices. In 1996, for example, Congress passed the Marriage Protection Act, which allowed states to restrict homosexual marriages and not recognize those granted by other states. Lastly, the use of punishment often involves restricting and penalizing banned activity such as drug trafficking, tax fraud, and a host of other activities. The obvious objective of the government is to severely curtail, and hopefully eliminate, such unlawful practices by citizens.

CHAPTER 15
FOREIGN POLICY: RELATIONS IN A DIVERSE WORLD

I.   Summary

There has been a historic shift in American foreign policy from the inception of the republic to the present time. With some exceptions, isolationism was the dominant foreign policy from 1789 to World War II. Since then, the policy of interventionism has dominated foreign policy decision makers in the United States. Both the president and Congress are allocated foreign affairs responsibilities in the Constitution, but the president clearly dominates the policy process. The president has much more resources at his/her disposal than the typical member of Congress–a national security advisor and several interrelated sets of agencies focusing on diplomacy, defense, and intelligence including the Departments of State and Defense as well as the Central Intelligence Agency. A number of international organizations also affect U.S. foreign policy. Those chairing or sitting on relevant committees in Congress can also wield a great deal of influence. In addition, a growing number of groups and interests also help to shape or influence foreign policy, including public opinion, the media, political parties, interest groups, and think tanks. The result is that the foreign policy process tends to be increasingly fragmented and hyperpluralistic, but much less so than domestic policy making.

II.   Outline

III. Key Terms, Concepts, Events, and People

Be able to identify and/or define each of the following and state its importance in a short paragraph.

Foreign policy (p.412)

Sovereignty (p.412)

Diplomacy (p.412)

Economic means (p.413)

Intelligence (p.413)

Military power (p.413)

International political system (p.413)

Multipolar (p.414)

Bipolar (p.414)

Unipolar (p.414)

Nongovernmental organizations (NGOs) (p.414)

Isolationism (p.414)

Interventionism (p.414)

Monroe Doctrine (p.414)

Expansionism (p.415)

Truman Doctrine (p.416)

Domino theory (p.416)

Cold War (p.416)

McCarthyism (p.416)

Vietnam Syndrome (p.416)

Détente (p.417)

Strategic Arms Limitation Talks (SALT) (p.417)

New world order (p.417)

Unilateralism (p.417)

Multilateral (p.417)

War Powers Act of 1973 (p.419)

Gulf of Tonkin Resolution (1964) (p.419)

Carter Doctrine (p.419)

Reagan Doctrine (p.419)

Diplomatic recognition (p.420)

Derecognition (p.420)

Executive agreements (p.420)

Intermistic issues (p.430)

Public diplomacy (p.431)

Domestic military (p.431)

Internal prosperity (p.434)

Selective militarism (p.435)

Pragmatic humanitarianism (p.435)

IV. Practice Exam

(Answers appear at the end of this chapter)

Multiple Choice

1. As of 1999, there were _____ members of
    the United Nations.
    A. 54
    B. 67
    C. 185
    D. 647

2. _____ espoused isolationism in
    1796.
    A. George Washington
    B. James Madison
    C. James Monroe
    D. Andrew Jackson

3. Because of _____, the United
    States acquired vast portions of the
    Southwest and California.
    A. the Civil War
    B. the Spanish American War
    C. War with the Barbary States
    D. the Mexican War

4. The _____ resulted in the
    acquisition or at least temporary control of
    Guam, Puerto Rico, Cuba, and the
    Philippines.
    A. War of 1812
    B. Mexican War
    C. Spanish American War
    D. Russo-Japanese War

5. The communists took control of mainland
    China in _____.
    A. 1898
    B. 1917
    C. 1949
    D. 1968

6. The dominant foreign policy from the late
    1940s to the early 1990s was
    A. containment.
    B. détente.
    C. isolationism.
    D. the domino theory.

7.	About _____ Americans lost their lives in Vietnam.
   A.	8,800
   B.	22,500
   C.	40,000
   D.	58,000

8.	_____ normalized relations with the People's Republic of China.
   A.	Lyndon Johnson
   B.	Jimmy Carter
   C.	Richard Nixon
   D.	Gerald Ford

9.	The Union of Soviet Socialist Republics dissolved in _____.
   A.	1978
   B.	1985
   C.	1991
   D.	1995

10.	_____ formally recognized communist-controlled Vietnam.
   A.	Gerald Ford
   B.	Jimmy Carter
   C.	Ronald Reagan
   D.	Bill Clinton

11.	Which one of the following is NOT part of the National Security Council?
   A.	President
   B.	Vice president
   C.	Secretary of State
   D.	Speaker of the U.S. House of Representatives

12.	Spending on foreign aid accounts for about _____ percent of the federal budget.
   A.	0
   B.	1
   C.	10
   D.	25

13.	Which one of the following is NOT one of the permanent members of the United Nations Security Council?
   A.	The United States
   B.	Germany
   C.	France
   D.	China

14.	_____ warned of the dangers inherent in the military-industrial complex.
   A.	Franklin Roosevelt
   B.	Harry Truman
   C.	Dwight Eisenhower
   D.	John Kennedy

15.	_____ opposed passage of the North American Free Trade Agreement (NAFTA).
   A.	Bill Clinton
   B.	Most Republicans
   C.	Pro-labor Democrats
   D.	George Bush

16.	_____ was very influential during the Reagan Administration.
   A.	The Brookings Institution
   B.	The Heritage Foundation
   C.	The Institute for Policy Studies
   D.	Amnesty International

17.	The first female secretary of state in U.S. history was_____.
   A.	Janet Reno
   B.	Madeleine Albright
   C.	Carol Browner
   D.	Ruth Bader Ginsburg

18.	Which of the following statements is TRUE?
   A.	35,000 women were deployed in Saudi Arabia prior to and during the Persian Gulf War.
   B.	One study concluded that 22 percent of all women in the U.S. Army have been sexually harassed the previous year.
   C.	George Bush supported lifting the ban on gays in the military.
   D.	Both a + b

19.	_____ declared that the Soviet Union was an "evil empire."
   A.	John Kennedy
   B.	Richard Nixon
   C.	Jimmy Carter
   D.	Ronald Reagan

20.   The most popular destination for
        immigrants coming to the United States is
        the state of
        A.   California.
        B.   Massachusetts.
        C.   New York.
        D.   Arizona.

Essays

21.   What instruments do nation-states use in furthering their own foreign policies? Explain.

22.   What lessons did policy makers learn as a result of the Vietnam War? Explain.

23.   Explain how presidents today can act relatively independently in foreign policy making.

24.   With fewer external threats today than during the Cold War, what two major questions currently confront
        policy makers in foreign affairs? Be sure to explain each one.

25.   According to foreign policy scholars, what four priorities should be pursued in American foreign policy?
        Explain.

V.   Critical Thinking Exercises

1.   In order to improve your knowledge of world geography, divide the world into its seven continents and
        learn where all the nation-states are located. Start with Antarctica, and then move on the following:
        Africa, Asia, Australia, Europe, North America, and South America.

2.   After improving your knowledge of global geography, select one nation state that you know little, or
        nothing, about. Conduct some research, and determine the history of the nation, as well as the state of its
        contemporary society and politics.

VI.   Answers to the Practice Exam

1.	C	11.	D
2.	A	12.	B
3.	D	13.	B
4.	C	14.	C
5.	C	15.	C
6.	A	16.	B
7.	D	17.	B
8.	B	18.	D
9.	C	19.	D
10.	D	20.	A

21.   Nation-states utilize several instruments in furthering their own foreign policies. First, they use
        diplomacy to interact peacefully with other nations. Second, they employ various economic means, such
        as trade regulations, tariffs, and economic assistance. Third, they engage in intelligence gathering. This
        allows them to better understand what other nations may or may not be doing in terms of activities.
        Another instrument is overt military power, including war or the threat of war. This is the ultimate tool of

foreign policy. Most nations use war to defend themselves from external attack. Some may use it to advance their national interest beyond their own borders.

22.   The lessons learned from Vietnam were numerous. First, Americans learned that their military power had limitations–that even a superpower could not necessarily win a war at any time or place, even against a fairly weak opponent. Second, policy makers learned that public opinion ultimately determines the price that people are willing to pay to fight communism or implement any foreign policy for that matter. Third, Vietnam taught policy makers that foreign policy would now be a shared process between the foreign policy elites in the executive branch, Congress, the mass media, interest groups, political parties, think tanks, and the people. The presidency lost power concerning foreign policy as a result of Vietnam, thus leading to the democratization of foreign affairs. Fourth, no longer would there be a broad, fundamental consensus on defining the very nature of American national interest, a consensus on which decades of foreign policy had been built.

23.   Today, presidents can act relatively independently in foreign policy making in a number of areas: (1) they can shift overall foreign policy direction by the statements they make; (2) they can imprint their preferences in treaties, from negotiating treaty detail to campaigning for their ratification; (3) they can initiate or terminate relations with other nations via their constitutional powers; (4) they can enter into executive agreements with other nation-states, which do not require the advice and consent of the U.S. Senate; (5) they can engage in personal diplomacy by dealing directly with other heads of state; and (6) they can make war by committing military resources to hostile places.

24.   Contemporary American foreign policy makers are confronted by two major questions in foreign affairs. The first is how large and combat ready should American forces be? Traditional military policy called for a military prepared to fight two wars at once. In today's smaller world characterized by more localized conflicts, is that standard still appropriate and judicious? Policy makers have not achieved a consensus on this issue. Second, to what extent should the military mirror the diversity of the American population? Racial discrimination has always been an issue in military history. Today, other groups are also asserting themselves and attempting to achieve equality in the military, including women and gays.

25.   According to many experts in foreign affairs, today's foreign policy should interweave four priorities–internal prosperity, global capitalism, selective militarism, and pragmatic humanitarianism. A first priority is internal prosperity. The internal strength is a nation's most important asset and economic prosperity is crucial in this endeavor. To build and maintain internal prosperity, the U.S. has attempted to remain competitive in the world political economy. A second priority is to spread democracy to other nations, and many believe that this requires the cultivation of capitalism. Global capitalism can open markets in other countries and essentially open their societies as well. A third priority is selective militarism. Advocates of this perspective believe that military interventionism should be reserved for protecting America's strategic and material interests. A fourth priority is pragmatic humanitarianism. Although selective militarism seems to be the policy of the future, there will always be a commitment to alleviate human suffering in the world. Military intervention may be required to do this, but not always because not all human suffering is the result of the ravages of war.